THE GERMANS WE TRUSTED

Stories of Friendship resulting

from the Second World War

Pamela Howe Taylor

The Lutterworth Press

The Lutterworth Press
P.O. Box 60
Cambridge
CB1 2NT

www.lutterworth.com
publishing@lutterworth.com

First Published in 2003

ISBN 0 7188 3034 2

British Library Cataloguing in Publication Data
A catalogue record is available from the British Library

Front Cover. Designed by Lawrence Taylor, featuring (left to right, top to bottom) 1. Kurt Geibel 2. Ernst Siebels 3. Artur Gernt 4. Horst Alexander 5. Willie Stracke, Heinz Schallenbach, Heiner Scherer 6. Karl Hunn 7. Fritz Kübler 8. Günther Scheffler 9. Fritz Defèr 10. Johannes Baumann 11. Geiert Meier 12. Christoph Gaudlitz

Printed in the United Kingdom by
Athenaeum Press

Contents

Foreword
By The Rt Hon Lord Hurd of Westwell
CH, CBE, PC

Since the last War we have seen the birth of a completely new democratic and friendly Germany. Thousands of British people have a direct experience of this. It is true that not enough of us yet know German, or study at German universities or even visit Germany. By contrast German students come here in large numbers, and German newspapers contain much more British news than our papers write about Germany. So there is some way to go before we make the most of this new friendship, but at least it is underway.

Rightly, we draw a sharp line between the new Germany and the Nazi Germany against which we fought for six years. We know more now than we did during the War about the horrors of Nazi rule and their persecution of other peoples, particularly the Jews. Something went terribly wrong, and there can be no valid excuses.

But there is another side to the story, which helps to explain how it was possible for the Germans to recover so quickly and form part of the free and democratic Western world. Pamela Taylor's book is not in the least political. It does not dig into the whys and wherefores of Nazism. It simply shows in three dozen personal stories how individual German prisoners of war managed to establish relationships of trust and friendship with people in Britain with whom they became involved when they were here in camps. They responded as normal human beings to acts of recognition and kindness.

Pamela Taylor has checked these stories with great care to make sure that they are accurate. These are not remote stories, for the Germans concerned are the fathers and grandfathers of the Germans whom we and our children now meet day by day.

Friendship brings understanding, and understanding is helped forward by the stories in these pages.

Introduction

My own involvement with German prisoners of the Second World War was as a child in Lancashire. My father became British padre to a POW camp outside our town. The story of resulting friendships is told in my book, *Enemies Become Friends*, and in the BBC Timewatch programme, *The Germans We Kept*, as well as in the German television documentary film, *Wie aus Feinden Freunde werden* (How Enemies Became Friends), shown throughout Germany.

The book you are about to read brings together more than thirty stories never before published. They are tales of surprising trust, warmth and friendship between former members of the German armed forces and their so-called enemies of the Second World War. Some friendships were made when German prisoners were taken to USA and Canada while the war was still raging in Europe. Although May 1945 saw the end of that war, there were over 400,000 German prisoners in Britain in the following year, housed in about 1,500 camps and hostels. Fraternisation was not officially allowed until December 1946. Some men remained prisoners as late as the end of 1948 before at last being freed to return home, if they had a home to go to. Over 25,000 opted to stay in Britain.

I am exceedingly grateful to the many people who have told me their stories. They searched their attics, archives and albums to verify details and find treasured documents and photographs, which they then entrusted to me. The book has been five years in the making, and each story still moves me, however many times I read it. Yet these feelings are insignificant compared with the deep emotions experienced by those involved.

All war is to be abhorred, with its cruelty and tragic impact on the lives of innocent people. We therefore rejoice on hearing of good unexpectedly emerging. My hope is that these stories will play a small part in convincing all of us that what the world needs is not war and preparation for war. Instead we require individuals who have the insight to see their enemies as fellow members of the human race and the courage to act accordingly.

Pamela Howe Taylor
Honiton, Devon
England
2003

1. The Astonishing Coincidence

Mr Earle Walls of Skipton, West Yorkshire, was in the family business of canal haulage. When the Second World War ended he answered a request for people with knowledge of inland waterways to go to Germany to assist in the clearing of rivers and canals. Many of the German waterways had been rendered unusable by bombed bridges and other wartime debris, but it was essential, for the reconstruction of the country, that their viability be restored for merchant shipping.

For Earle, taking the job in Germany meant leaving his wife Dorothy and their daughter Margaret at home in Skipton. His father and two younger brothers had to continue running the family business, Walls Shipping Ltd, without him. After a short time in Germany, Earle obtained the position of Chief Director of Inland Waterways for the British Control Commission, covering the area of the Rhine North to the Kiel Canal in the British and American Zones. This was a high-profile post that demanded some considerable degree of security. Earle was not supposed to drive alone or even drive himself. The allocation of a chauffeur to him was said to be both for convenience and for safety. Nor was he ever supposed to give lifts to German civilians.

One wild and rainy December night, for reasons known only to himself, he broke the regulations on all three counts. Driving home alone from a meeting, he passed a stooping man, struggling against the elements. Pulling up, he offered the man a lift, telling him he was going as far as Duisburg. The man got into the car, but conversation was limited because neither man spoke the other's language well. The German man managed to make Earle understand where he lived and told him his name, Herr Janisch. Just before getting out of the car, he said he had a son in a prisoner of war camp in England. When Earle enquired his whereabouts, imagine his astonishment to be told "Skipton"! On hearing that Skipton was actually Earle's home-town, Herr Janisch was equally amazed.

Overdale POW Camp was on the northeast outskirts of Skipton beyond Skipton Castle on the road to Bolton Abbey. Groups of prisoners could sometimes be seen working in the fields, and crocodiles of young men in drab clothing were escorted, from time to time, through the town centre on their way between the camp and the railway station, no doubt being moved from camp to camp.

News of the almost unbelievable coincidental meeting near Duisburg spread fast, reaching Skipton before Christmas. Mr and Mrs Walls' daughter Margaret, then ten years of age, remembers how a prisoner arrived unexpectedly on their doorstep on Christmas Day itself, a great surprise. He was Wolfgang Janisch. Thus a new friendship began. After this first visit, although restrictions at Overdale Camp at this time allowed men out on their own only infrequently, Wolfgang visited the Walls family for a Sunday afternoon or evening whenever he could, bringing with him a friend, Helmut Kunkhe. "These visits inevitably included a huge Sunday lunch or evening meal cooked by my mother," Margaret now recalls, "before they returned to the camp with whatever other goodies they were allowed to take back! They were marvellous to her in return, whilst my father was away, doing the gardening and other heavy jobs around the house in return for good Yorkshire hospitality and the opportunity to spend some time in a homely environment."

That year Margaret and her mother Dorothy went to spend the seven weeks of the school summer holidays with her father who was then living near Bielefeld. Margaret still has vivid memories of the devastation she saw in Duisburg, Essen and other industrial cities they visited. Many people were living in what had previously been their cellars, because

Helmut Kunkhe, Margaret Walls, a school friend and Wolfgang Janisch

Wolfgang Janisch, with Dorothy and Margaret Walls outside their Skipton home, 1947

everything above ground had been flattened during the war. The conditions made a deep impression on the ten-year-old girl. They visited Wolfgang's parents, Herr and Frau Janisch, who were thrilled to see them, to hear first-hand news of their son and, hardly less important, to receive such things as tea, coffee and chocolate from British Services' supplies. These goods were normally unobtainable by the German population whose diet at this time was far from adequate. From then on, whenever Earle returned to Germany after a spell of leave, he would be dispatched with huge food parcels to take to Herr and Frau Janisch.

One of the German maids who kept house for Earle in Bielefeld, a very attractive German woman, went later to work for the Walls family in Skipton. She subsequently married a tenor from the local Gilbert and Sullivan Society and settled in Skipton for a time before deciding to return home to Germany.

The consequences of that astonishingly coincidental meeting between two men on a wet and windy evening in Germany lasted longer than anyone could have guessed. Dorothy Walls started to write letters to Mr and Mrs Janisch even while their son remained at Overdale Camp. After his repatriation, she sent parcels and letters to Wolfgang and to Helmut also. In fact, she kept up correspondence with the Janisch family (using English and a little German) for almost forty years.

2. Windows of East Chinnock

If you travel the road from Yeovil to Crewkerne in Somerset you will pass the Parish Church of St Mary the Virgin in East Chinnock. Parts of the building date back to the fifteenth century, and the site housed an earlier Norman church. What might be of special interest to the visitor are some twentieth-century additions, the stained-glass windows. They have an unexpected story to tell.

Günther Anton was a young rear gunner in the German Luftwaffe in 1944, when, at the age of 18, his plane was shot down over Southampton. He parachuted to the ground safely but was taken prisoner. At a POW camp in Douglas on the Isle of Man he met Anton ("Tony") Bischoff who had been taken prisoner in the Netherlands by British paratroopers. The two young men were to become lifelong friends. When the war ended they were both moved to Houndstone Camp near Yeovil in Somerset.

Each day the prisoners went to work on farms around Yeovil, and Günther was often sent to Bridge Farm and Old Court Farm in East Chinnock, a village of about 400 inhabitants only a few miles from the camp. From the fields of these farms he could look down on the attractive Parish Church of St Mary. As a young man, not yet 20 years of age, he was very concerned for the safety of his parents who had been living in eastern Europe in Silesia. One day he decided to call into the church to rest and pray. He found tranquillity there amidst his anxieties. Günther often returned to the church, and he always found hope and comfort.

St Mary's Church, East Chinnock
(photo: Brenda Bickerton)

The people of East Chinnock were thankful that the 29 people from their village who served in the war had all returned safely. Now they had German prisoners in their midst, and some villagers invited those who worked on the farms to visit them and their families at weekends. Günther was appreciative of the friendship offered to him by people in East Chinnock such as Arthur and Margaret Fry of Bridge Farm and Rev. G.F. Raban, the Rector of the church.

Meanwhile Günther's friend Tony Bischoff was working on a farm in nearby Brympton where he became friendly with the farmer, Mr Diment, his wife and their three teenage children. Each working day he was allowed to go into the farm kitchen to eat his lunch. The more Mrs Flora Diment got to know Tony the more she became like a mother to him, serving him tea and cake at the end of the day, and giving him the *Daily Mail* newspaper to take back to the camp. She spoke such clear English that fifty-five years later Herr Bischoff recalled, "She was for me the best English teacher."

At the camp a choir was formed which both Günther and Tony joined. This 15 strong male voice choir was asked to sing in Anglican and Roman Catholic churches in the area, and this became another way in which friendships with local people were formed.

On Günther's many visits to East Chinnock Church to pray for the safety of his parents, he could not fail to notice the stained glass window at the east end, given in memory of a church warden from the nineteenth century. It was the only coloured window in the church: all the others were of plain glass. The east window was of particular interest to Günther because his own father was a Master Glazier. Gradually, the imaginative idea of making a new stained-glass window for the church began to form in his mind. When he at last heard that his parents were safe he felt that the creation of a window would be an act of thanksgiving as well as a sign of peace between the two nations.

When Günther was eventually released in 1948, his parents had moved west to Leonberg near Stuttgart and set up business there. He joined his father in the business of making high quality stained glass, and eventually he too became a Master Glazier. Günther told his father about his idea for East Chinnock Church, to replace one of the plain windows with a beautifully coloured one. For some years nothing was done about it, but, just before his death, Herr Anton senior reminded his son, "Do not forget about the window for East Chinnock."

In his spare time, Günther started work on a window depicting scenes from Christ's life. It was to be 14 feet high to fit a position in the south wall of the nave of East Chinnock Church. In 1962, 14 years after he had left Somerset, he and Tony Bischoff and their wives set off for England. They arrived at Bridge Farm in East Chinnock with the window in 12 sections in the boot of their car. The two ladies made sure each piece of glass was perfectly clean, the men pieced it all together, and at last the window was installed in the south wall of the church, near the chancel. It shone out as a wonderful tribute to the help and comfort the church had given Günther as a young man a long way from home, and it was also seen as a symbol of thanksgiving for the friendship shown to German prisoners by the people in the area (see colour photographs).

Günther Anton and Tony Bischoff installing the first window at East Chinnock in 1962

Günther told the churchwardens, "Now I want to fill your church with my windows." It seems that he felt that this gift, marvellous though it was, was not sufficient as a thanksgiving to God for his safe return from war and as a symbol of reconciliation between former enemies. At home he started work on another window, this time to fit a position in the north sanctuary. When finished, this window depicted the infant Jesus and Christ the King. In June 1967 Günther, Tony and their wives, Elfriede and Elisabeth, again visited East Chinnock, accompanied this time by Josef Vees, the designer of the windows. They fitted this second window opposite the first one, both being signed by Günther Anton and Josef Vees. As they worked, Günther said, "I want to put in four or five more windows, but it will take years." At a service attended by the German visitors on the following Sunday the two windows were dedicated by the Ven. J. du B. Lance, Archdeacon of Wells

Günther's determination to make more windows for East Chinnock did not abate. After two further years he had prepared glass for

Tony Bischoff and Günther Anton with Rev. Percy Nichols, Rector of East Chinnock, in 1962

three smaller windows in the chancel. One showed the archangels Gabriel and Michael, and another pictured Raphael and Uriel (see colour photographs). The third window depicted three of Christ's miracles: the healing of a lame man, the woman who touched the hem of his robe and the raising of Jairus's daughter. Günther sent the glass for these windows to England ahead of his next visit, but the consignment ran into difficulties. Apparently Customs and Excise officials could not believe it was a gift. The glass was confiscated, and questions were asked. In due course, however, it was released, and the windows were installed.

It was thirteen years later in July 1982 that Günther next visited England bringing four more windows, showing other scenes from the life of Christ and the Virgin Mary. This time, Günther and Elfriede brought their younger daughter, Silke; and Tony's sister, Erika Henn, came too with her husband, Leo, and son, Thomas. Leo and Thomas Henn were both strong workmen, having a painting and decorating business in Neckarsulm, north of Stuttgart, and they were a great help with the large task of fitting so many windows on this visit. When the sun shone through these new windows they were glorious. Mr Arthur Fry from Bridge Farm, one of Günther's oldest East Chinnock friends, was quoted in the press as saying,

> It would have cost nearly £10,000 to put in these last four. They are made up of 6,000 pieces of glass. All the Germans who worked here [as prisoners] were very popular and hard-working. We have been friends ever since, and when I went to Germany last year, the feeling there was tremendous. Everyone was saying there should never be another war.

The following Sunday the new windows were dedicated by Rev. Percy Nichols who had been Rector of East Chinnock during the period of the installation of the first five windows, and who had himself been a prisoner of war in Italy.

1982 newspaper report showing Günther Anton and Tony Bischoff fitting one of the last windows. (Bristol Evening Post)

Before returning to Germany, Leo and Thomas Henn took down the weather vane cock from the top of the church tower, Thomas standing precariously on a parapet to reach it. They took it home where they re-gilded it in their workshop before returning it to be replaced where it belonged and can still be seen.

Thomas Henn renovating the steeple cock in his workshop in Germany, 1982

The German visitors had stayed with families in the village, and as a result some new Anglo-German friendships were born. For example, Erika and Leo Henn had stayed with John and Mary White. The following year Mr and Mrs White and their daughter went to stay with Herr and Frau Henn in Neckarsulm, and since then have kept up the friendship. Indeed, an unofficial link was developing between East Chinnock and the village of Dahenfeld near Neckarsulm (where Tony Bischoff also lived), involving the Mayor of Dahenfeld, Herr Hugo Keicher, who twice visited East Chinnock with his wife and daughter.

In May 1986 about 35 people from East Chinnock travelled to Dahenfeld and Neckarsulm for an excellent five-day visit arranged by Herr Bischoff. This included a town hall reception, a dinner with the municipal council, a party with a choir and band, and Mass in the village church. There were also sightseeing trips to see works of art, a car factory, a bicycle museum, vineyards, Bavarian historic buildings, and of course a visit to Leonberg to see Günther Anton's workshop. The verdict was that, although the visitors had been run off their feet with almost every spare moment organised, they had had a wonderful time, being treated very generously by their kind German friends. One of the letters written from Somerset to Germany afterwards read, "It was a privilege to be made so welcome everywhere and in those few days to see so much of your lovely town and countryside and to meet such friendly and welcoming people. It was not only a wonderful holiday for me but also a very meaningful experience." The writer adds that the East Chinnock windows, the story behind them and the continuing friendships over the years, have been a great source of joy and encouragement.

A year later, Tony Bischoff arranged for a large party to spend a week in East Chinnock, all staying in private homes. There were 17 former prisoners of Houndstone Camp, with wives and families, and a few other people from his home-town of Neckarsulm. Due to travel delays they arrived at one o'clock in the morning, but the people of East

Chinnock were there to meet them. Lay Reader Jim Cranton and his wife Daphne were hosts to Ernst and Gertrude ("Trude") Erb of Offenburg, beginning another completely new friendship. As a prisoner, Ernst had worked at a farm in the village of Tintinhull, north of East Chinnock, owned by Farmer Clements. Ernst remembered giving the farmer a box he had carved, and now discovered that the son of the family, Peter Clements, still had the box. Jim and Daphne Cranton were invited to Offenburg in subsequent years to stay with Ernst and Trude. Despite Ernst's death a few years ago, they still maintain the link with Trude and her friends.

During the 1987 visit, the then vicar, Rev. Richard Cloete, presented Günther with a photograph of the church as a token of thanks for all he had done over the last 25 years since the first window was installed in the church. With the nine windows now given by Günther, the Parish Church of St Mary the Virgin, East Chinnock, at last had a complete set of stained glass windows. Even so, it was to receive yet another gift from the former prisoner of war. Next to the south door is an arch dividing the nave from the bell tower. Günther made a stained glass picture of the Agnus Dei (Lamb of God) and superimposed it on glass bricks to be fitted into the space under the arch. First it was necessary to brick up part of the arch. In 1988, when Günther was aged 62, he and his wife came to East Chinnock again with three other former prisoners of Houndstone Camp. They worked on the bricking up of the arch followed by the installation of the glass bricks and the Agnus Dei picture (see colour photographs). This was the final instalment of Günther's 30 years of work for the church. Local television reported that the set of windows would grace any cathedral, calling them a "gift beyond price". Günther told the television interviewer that he had done this work for his friends in England, for friendship between English and German people and for peace in all the world. Shortly after his return home he sent a plaque which was placed at the side of the new screen. It reads:

In memory of our common work
as a little share for peace in the world
4 ex-POWs Houndstone Camp 1945-1948
Günther Anton 7250 Leonberg – Stuttgart
Ernst Erb 7600 Offenburg
Heinrich Bauscher 6456 Langenselbold
Heinz Schöps 4952 Porta-Westfalica
June 1988

(The numbers are the towns' post codes and not the men's POW numbers!)

In May of the following year, Günther paid one final visit to Somerset for a special service of dedication and thanksgiving. The church was packed with about 200 people including a number of Germans who had come for the weekend from Dahenfeld. This was to be no ordinary occasion.

Herr Günther Anton, the Right Rev. George Carey and
Mr Paddy Ashdown MP at the Dedication Service, 1989
(photo: Brenda Bickerton)

Singers from the choirs of the nearby villages of West Coker and Hardington were to swell the East Chinnock choir, making it necessary for a tent to be erected in the church yard in which they could robe and disrobe, leaving the church vestry for the visiting dignitaries. As there was no rector at that time, the service was to be conducted by Lay Reader Jim Cranton, but two former rectors of the church were to be present, Revs Percy Nichols and Richard Cloete. The dedication and sermon were to be given by the Bishop of Bath and Wells, the Right Rev. George Carey (who was later to become Archbishop of Canterbury). The local Member of Parliament, Mr Paddy Ashdown, was to read the lesson, and also invited were the German Consul for Avon, Somerset and Gloucester, Mr John Langman; South Somerset District Council's Chairman, Councillor Jane Clark; and County Councillor Bill Drower who had himself been a prisoner of war in Japan.

On this auspicious occasion the Bishop started his address by saying the windows were absolutely stunning, remarking upon the design and great artistry involved. They were a sign of reconciliation and thus a contribution to peace in the world. He quoted the first verse of Psalm 103, "Bless the Lord, oh my soul, and forget not all his benefits". Despite being a prisoner, Günther Anton had not forgotten the benefits he had received in East Chinnock. The windows symbolised looking back with thanksgiving, looking out with hope and looking upwards with confidence.

Mr Paddy Ashdown MP said later that it was one of the most moving ceremonies he had ever taken part in. In the service he read from the book of Revelation about the author's vision of a new heaven and the new earth, and he had to pause before saying the words "He will wipe every tear from their eye", finding himself affected by the occasion. The same passage was then read in German by Pastor Heinz Becker, who had joined the party from Germany simply as a potential customer of Herr Anton's, to see examples of his work in the windows of East Chinnock. "As for the windows," wrote Paddy Ashdown the following week in the local newspaper, "they are a wonder. East Chinnock Church is one of the most charming in our area. There is a real feeling of happiness there which you can almost touch. But Günther Anton's windows have given colour and light and great beauty to it as well. Here is a practical symbol of one man's thanks to God and to people who gave him help at a time of need." Rev. Richard Cloete commented that Günther's generosity showed the great love he had for East Chinnock and also reflected the love the village people had shown towards him. "It is his little bit towards peace in the world today and in bringing people together", he added.

At a reception after the service a presentation was made to Günther by Mrs Rosemary Ottery whom Günther remembered as a toddler at Bridge Farm forty years before. On behalf of her own family she had made a framed scroll bearing the words in English and German, "Presented to Günther Anton to celebrate the friendship between our peoples and to further the cause of peace and reconciliation. The windows and screen were made, given and installed in our church by you between 1962 and 1988 and dedicated by the Right Reverend George Carey, Bishop of Bath and Wells on 20 May 1989." Depicted on the scroll were the shields of Somerset and Stuttgart. A barbecue was then held in the garden of the Portman Arms which has been described as a "wonderful international party". The events of this day were reported, not only locally, but also in several newspapers in Germany.

Bishop Carey must have been particularly impressed by what had happened as he invited

Rosemary Ottery, Günther and Elfriede Anton
with the framed scroll made by Rosemary
(photograph by Brenda Bickerton)

At the garden party following the dedication of the windows, 1989.
Seated (left to right): Andreas & Tony Bischoff, Elfriede Anton, Elfriede
Albers. Middle: Joan Boyers, Peter Clements, Ernst & Trude Erb, Heinz
Bruhn, Heinz Albers, another ex-prisoner, Daphne Cranton.
Back (middle to right): Heinz Becker, Günther Anton & Jim Cranton
(photo: Brenda Bickerton)

Günther and his family and friends to visit him in Wells on the following
Monday. A group of eight German and British people therefore travelled to
Wells and enjoyed morning coffee with the Bishop and his wife Eileen in
his palace, as well as a tour of the palace and its grounds. Later the Bishop
wrote personally to Günther in Germany.

One of the former prisoners in the German group was Heinz Bruhn,
who had been camp leader at Houndstone Camp. He had spent the intervening years at his home in East Germany and was not sure whether to
make this visit, having heard bad things about the British capitalist society.
However, he managed somehow to get out of East Germany for two weeks
with the help of a passport from West Germany and found it hard to
believe that he was in the free west for a short time. He proved to be a
very useful member of the group, acting as interpreter, and was moved
to tears on more than one occasion by the fellowship he experienced.

For Günther, this visit to East Chinnock was to be his last: he lived
for only a further six months. It seems that his important work had
been accomplished. In November 1989 eight people from the village flew
in a ten-seater chartered aircraft from Bournemouth Airport to Stuttgart
to attend Günther Anton's funeral. (They were Jim and Daphne Cranton,
Rev. Percy Nichols, Joan Boyers, Arthur and Muriel Harris, Ric Pallister
and Nick Weber, with two pilots.) Tony Bishoff arranged overnight
accommodation for them in Neckarsulm. The next day they went to the

Tony Bischoff and his granddaughter Christina with the British telephone kiosk installed in his garden in Germany

funeral, which was also attended by thirteen former war prisoners from Houndstone Camp, including those named on the church plaque. Six weeks later a service of thanksgiving for the life and work of Herr Günther Anton was held in St Mary's Church, East Chinnock.

But what of Günther's friend Tony Bischoff who had played such a large part in both the installation of the windows and also with the practical arrangements for the visits? Because of his love of England, he is described by some of his friends as half English. His career was as an electrician, but he was also a town councillor for 33 years in Neckarsulm. When he retired from the council at the age of 70, his fellow CDU councillors gave him a British red telephone kiosk as a present, which now adorns the garden of his house and is lit up at night. As well as his many trips to East Chinnock with Günther, he has been responsible for additional visits with his townspeople, including a group of town councillors who stayed in a local hotel in the spring of 1998. As well as sightseeing in Somerset and Dorset, these group visits usually included a reception in the village hall, an international party in the pub near the church and of course a service in the church itself. Tony is still in touch with Farmer Diment's children and grandchildren who have been to Neckarsulm to see him several times, and he and his family have often visited them in the Yeovil area.

Some players in the wartime story have now passed on. Other friendships continue and new ones are still being formed. Far into the future, the wonderful windows of East Chinnock Church will no doubt give pleasure, inspiration and cause for thought to many worshippers and visitors who admire them. They stand in the old Parish Church as majestic symbols of gratitude, friendship, peace and reconciliation between former enemies from a century which saw two devastating world wars. All this is due to the vision, determination, generosity and artistic skill of a young rear gunner in the German air force, who was shot down over Southampton.

3. Gifts Full of Memories

Mr and Mrs Harder and their four sons were one of a number of families who emigrated from the Ukraine to Canada in the early 1920s. They belonged to the Mennonite church, a Protestant denomination which originated in Europe in the sixteenth century, many of whose members had moved to the Ukraine. (In the eighteenth century, Catherine the Great of Russia, herself a German, had invited Mennonites from north Germany to move to the vast Steppes of the Ukraine to build up agriculture there, knowing them to be agricultural experts.) However, after the Russian revolution of 1917, many Mennonites left the Ukraine, fearing persecution because of their Christian faith under the new communist Soviet Union of which the Ukraine had become a part.

When the Harder family moved to Canada in 1924, they began farming in Manitoba, where two more sons were born. They and other such families were brought up in a strict German tradition which Mennonites had retained during their life in the Ukraine. They spoke German at home and on the farm, and their church services also were in German.

Mennonites have a history of being opposed to military service, so when the Second World War began, the adults of the church believed their sons should not become involved in the fighting. In any case, those whose families had emigrated from the Ukraine felt more German than Russian, and the thought of fighting against Germans was especially unacceptable to them. Furthermore, they had heard stories of their relatives and friends who had stayed in the Ukraine and suffered greatly under Communism. To help the Soviet Union seemed impossible to them. The advice to their sons was, therefore, to apply to be classed as conscientious objectors and find an alternative form of wartime service.

So it came about that George Harder, along with many other young men, was sent to work at a disused lumber camp in Alberta. In January 1941 at the age of 23, he could be found sawing logs into lengths suitable for use as props in local coal mines. After only two weeks of this work, however, he heard that the cook was looking for a helper in the kitchen, and so he started his career as a "flunkey", as they termed all such kitchen help.

The following year, a German POW camp was positioned about three miles from the lumber camp. Every day a truckload of prisoners, watched by half a dozen Canadian guards, were brought to the lumber camp's machine shop, which still had drills and lathes left behind by the previous owners. Many of the Germans were expert tradesmen, and in this machine shop they created many useful items of wooden furniture. Each morning a very young German prisoner, accompanied by a guard, came to the kitchen to collect a pot of boiling water to take back to his comrades in the machine shop, for making coffee. The Canadians were not supposed to talk to the German prisoners, but George said "Guten Morgen!" to the young man a few times, and once he realised that George really could speak his language there was no stopping him. He told George all about himself. His name was Erich, he was 16 years of age and the youngest prisoner in his camp. In the previous year, the German sail boat on which he was receiving training had been torpedoed by a British submarine in the North Sea. He had been captured and taken first to England and then brought to Canada.

Now that George and Erich had made contact with each other, Erich would return to the kitchen after delivering the hot water each morning and talk to George, who was usually peeling potatoes. Sometimes George would find an apple or orange for him, a treat for a prisoner at that time. Soon Erich began to look upon George almost as an older brother, and George became very fond of him. On one occasion Erich presented him with a ship in a bottle which he and his friends had made in their free time. It was a wonderful gift (see colour photographs). But then something went wrong.

The guards who looked after the prisoners were Canadian First World War veterans. Some were rather old and had difficulty climbing in and out of the large army trucks in which the prisoners were transported. On one occasion George saw a truck arriving and could hardly believe his eyes. The prisoners quickly jumped down from the back of the truck. Then the guards, instead of jumping down after them, first handed their rifles down to the prisoners to hold while they descended from the truck more slowly. Small wonder, then, that a decision was made to rotate the guards between POW camps every three months, to prevent them becoming too casual with the prisoners.

One morning, Erich came for the water as usual but with a new guard who looked hard at George during the usual German conversation. That afternoon George was called to the supervisor's office where the commanding officer of the guard detail was also present. George was asked to explain why he was talking to a prisoner in German. After a lengthy interview, in which he tried to convince them that he was not a spy, he was ordered never to speak to the prisoners again. When Erich came to the kitchen the next morning he started speaking to George as usual, but George kept shaking his head until Erich realised something was wrong. After that Erich was upset and stayed away from the kitchen.

George's working hours were long. He started work at five in the morning, but he had a break in the afternoon before supper time. As the weather became slightly warmer towards spring, George would go for a walk in the afternoon, sometimes borrowing the cook's fishing rod. A mile up river was a small waterfall, and here a few trout could be caught. One afternoon he noticed a white-haired man in POW uniform sitting by the river with no guard, and George guessed who he might be from something Erich had told him. He approached the man and spoke to him in German, which took him by surprise. The man quickly introduced himself as Hans Meyer, the captain of a German passenger liner which had been confiscated in New York harbour when the United States entered the war in December 1941. At that time the Americans were not equipped to handle prisoners of war so the Captain and his crew were handed over to the Canadians. Although they were really civilian internees rather than military prisoners they were sent to POW camps in Canada. As the oldest of the 400 internees, Captain Meyer was permitted to wander outside the prison camp, having given his word of honour that he would not try to escape. He was the only person to be given this privilege.

In his conversation with the Captain, George asked if he knew Erich and was told, "Yes, everyone knows Erich, because he is the youngest man in our camp". George explained what had happened in the kitchen and added that he missed Erich's morning visits. Captain Meyer had already heard Erich's side of the story. Erich's feelings had been hurt,

*George Harder with the mattress cover given
to him by Captain Hans Meyer*

thinking that George did not talk to him because he was angry with him for some reason. The Captain promised to explain the actual reason to Erich, and he must have succeeded in his explanation, because next morning Erich was back in the kitchen again. There were new guards by now, and fortunately they were friendly and on speaking terms with everyone.

In addition to furthering his friendship with Erich each morning, George also had the opportunity to see Captain Meyer some afternoons at the quiet spot by the river. The Captain's ship had travelled regularly from Hamburg to Cherbourg to Southampton to New York and back again. When it was taken by the Americans in New York harbour, Captain Meyer had been able to keep only one single memento from his ship, a mattress cover in which to carry his personal belongings. One day he brought this mattress cover to the meeting place by the river and gave it to George, telling him he wanted him to have it as a reminder of their friendship.

George Harder has kept the mattress cover from Captain Hans Meyer and also the ship in the bottle from Erich. He has preserved both these gifts with great care for nearly sixty years. For him they carry many memories of the two unusual friendships, memories which, he says, still remain highlights of his wartime experiences in Canada.

4. Prisoner for a Reason

When Horst Alexander joined the German air force in July 1944 at the age of 17 he could not have known how important it would be that he should become a prisoner of war in England. In November 1944, like many fellow countrymen, he was captured and held in Belgium. Although it was a relatively mild winter, Horst often woke up with his legs covered in snow because of insufficient room in the shelter for his whole body. Then, in March 1945, he and his comrades were herded onto a ship. They spent hours sitting on rusty piping or lying on the floor of the ship as it crossed the Channel from Ostend to Tilbury.

It was a pleasant spring morning when Horst arrived in England aged just 18 years. The morning air was suddenly shattered by a wailing noise of many sirens, precisely the same noise he had heard many times at home before running to the nearest air-raid shelter. Two V1 rockets were approaching London, and the detonation of one of them could still be heard. The men hoped they would not be harmed by their own comrades. Fortunately things began to improve for Horst and his fellow prisoners in London. For the first time for many months they were able to have a shower with plenty of soap, and new underwear and a good pair of second-hand boots were allocated to them. Their meals were served in big tents with tables and benches, and they slept in clean tents on dry straw mats. The biggest surprise was that their guards were willing to talk to them and answer their questions. From early childhood they had been indoctrinated with National Socialism and believed that, beyond German borders, hostility and inhumanity were all that could be expected. Now they began to realise that people across the sea were human beings too.

Among the British soldiers interviewing each prisoner were some who spoke German so fluently that it seemed as though they must have learned the language in Hamburg, Frankfurt-am-Main or Berlin. It turned out that they were Jews, born in Germany, now serving in the British army and putting their knowledge of the German language to good use. Horst had not known much about Jews prior to this. He remembered one day as a boy of 14, visiting his father, a police officer, in the police station of his home-town. There he saw a man wearing a large yellow star on his jacket. His father had reluctantly told him that the man was a Jewish cobbler, and Jews had to report to the police station regularly.

As a prisoner of war in Britain, Horst was moved about the country and experienced various POW camps. However, on three occasions he was sent with a small group of prisoners to spend a few days in a very large deserted country house. He learnt later that these visits were to deter squatters. The well-equipped mansions

Horst Alexander, front row, second from right, and other prisoners at Featherstone Park Camp, Haltwhistle, Northumberland in 1945

were remarkable. One had six bathrooms and the men spent almost the whole of the first night in the bath tubs. During the day they enjoyed sliding down the marble banisters, making up for boyish experiences they had missed for years. As Horst points out, "There are no tubs nor banisters in huts!"

One of Horst's worst memories of these times was in the summer of 1946 when he was at Featherstone Park Camp in Haltwhistle, Northumberland. A letter arrived from his father in Germany telling him that his mother, his sister and her little son Axel, Horst's nephew, had all been killed on 16 April 1945 as the Soviet Army invaded Germany. This information had taken over a year to reach Horst. He knew that his brother had previously been killed in action in April 1942; now Horst and his father were the only survivors of their family.

Soon after the war ended all prisoners had been confronted with the depressing pictures and descriptions of conditions found when German concentration camps were discovered. The aims and beliefs of National Socialism had completely broken down, and with it had gone many of Horst's ideals. From this time he started searching for alternative beliefs and read German philosophers such as Schopenhauer and Kant, and this he did for about a year prior to his move to the Wirral peninsular, south of Liverpool.

On 11th December 1946 Horst was moved to Clatterbridge Camp, near Bebington in the Wirral, a camp of only about 120 prisoners. Every week-day they were occupied in pulling down old Nissen huts, erected years before on the estate of Lord Leverhume. At weekends the prisoners were glad of a change of scenery, and Horst found his way more than once to the museum in Port Sunlight where interesting old furniture could be seen, such as a bed in which Napoleon was said to have slept. On one such visit, Lord Leverhume himself happened to come to the museum at the same time. Horst was somewhat surprised to find himself as the only other person in the room apart from two assistants who were bowing a little as they spoke to the aristocratic gentleman. Horst felt a little out of place in his POW garb as he similarly made a few bows, not knowing what else to do! As he left the museum he caught his first glimpse of a Rolls Royce motor car.

The place which was easiest for the prisoners to visit was the small town of Bebington, about 45 minutes walk from the camp. Horst got to know the area well and noticed that one building had the name "Bethesda" inscribed prominently on the end wall, though it did not mean anything to him. However, at Christmas an invitation was received in the camp for anyone who wished to go to Bethesda Hall for a cup of coffee (not tea) on Friday 27 December at 5 o'clock. Persons interested were to give their names to the camp clerk so that Mr Bennington, the person who had issued the invitation, would know how many to expect. Horst remembers this invitation being discussed among the prisoners, but for quite a number "it had the smell of the attempt to exert religious influence". Eleven men decided to give their names to the clerk.

At 5 o'clock on the Friday in question, Horst was extremely surprised to find that the number had swelled. Scores of men were arriving at Bethesda Hall. In the end 80 prisoners turned up. With no adverse reaction to the unexpectedly large number of guests, the hosts very quickly arranged additional tables and benches as well as cups and saucers. Before long everyone had a seat, and coffee and cakes were served in abundance.

Mr Bennington, his wife and the other church members all seemed to be cheerful, radiating kindness and openness, an attitude which the prisoners had not really expected. The men were asked to sing German Christmas carols, while Mrs Bennington came round with more cake and coffee. She spoke to them in German, and it was German with a pure Saxon accent, a familiar sound to some of the men.

Gradually the visitors discovered that Mr and Mrs Bennington were Germans. He was a trained engineer, who had owned an electrical appliance company in Hamburg, but who had been driven out of Germany with his wife in 1938 because he was Jewish. A number of his relatives had been killed in German concentration camps. One of the prisoners present came from Hamburg, and Mr Bennington recognised the accent and embraced him as a fellow countryman.

The hosts all belonged to the Bethesda Assembly, a branch of the Open Brethren Christian denomination. They spoke of the love of God in Jesus Christ, a message not new to the men and perhaps not welcome to some. However, everything was presented in an acceptable way, with personal conversations, obvious warmth and affection, from people who only an hour before had been complete strangers. The men were amazed. Horst explains the prisoners' feelings as follows.

> We were a company of men more or less rough and ready, who for years had to live behind barbed wire, when suddenly we found ourselves sitting in English church rooms at tables laid for all of us, and being attended to by ever so kind civilians, who only two years ago had been our opponents in a terrible war.

On the way back to the camp many of the men discussed intently what they had experienced. It was a remarkable encounter for them all, but for Horst it was something astounding.

> Even now, although it is more than 50 years ago, I remember precisely these hours. I was totally soaked with perspiration and almost all the way back to the camp, a walk of about three quarters of an hour, I was shaking all over. I was hardly involved in the discussion. I think I was moved to such an extent I was incapable of talking much. The following night I could not sleep.

Horst's main fascination was with the attitude of these people. What had enabled them to overcome their natural human reaction when confronted by the enemy and to show such genuine kindness? He determined to find out more. From then on he attended not only the Sunday morning breaking of bread services at Bethesda but also Bible and prayer meetings on weekdays. He began to learn what "Open Brethren" were and became very friendly with other members of the Assembly, such as Harry and Elsie Dumbell and William and Rosa McMillan who invited him to their house many times. He read Christian literature very carefully and with great interest, by authors he had never heard of before, and he set himself the task of comparing the English and German translations of the Bible.

Of course, other prisoners wanted to continue the friendship begun on that Friday after Christmas. Mr and Mrs Bennington's

Horst Alexander as a POW in Mr and Mrs Dumbell's garden in 1947

flat was very often crowded with German prisoners who enjoyed the homely atmosphere. The rooms were so full of men that if Horst wanted a personal talk with Mr Bennington they had to go into the bedroom or the kitchen. It was during a quiet time together in the small kitchen of the flat that Horst accepted Jesus as his personal Saviour. A Jew had led a German into the Christian faith. Herr Alexander now regards this time in Bebington as "a special gift of God".

Five days before Horst was moved away from the Wirral to another camp, he had a different experience which he remembers well. On 19 April 1947 he visited the Philharmonic Hall in Liverpool to listen to Handel's *Messiah* conducted by Malcolm Sargent. Over the intervening years he has kept safely the programme of this wonderful event.

When the time for his move to another camp came, Horst found that his Bebington friends had already informed the local Assembly about him. On the first Sunday morning, Brethren picked him up at the gate of the new camp to be their guest for the day. Although they had never met each other before, Horst remembers that "the greeting was a hearty one as perhaps usual amongst relatives". This happened the next time he moved camp as well, so that his German comrades wondered how many uncles and aunts he had in England. It was at an Assembly in Worcester that he was baptised, together with another prisoner who had become a Christian.

After Horst's release, he naturally continued the contacts with his friends in Bebington who had played such a crucial role in his life in England. Over several decades many visits

LIVERPOOL WELSH
CHORAL UNION

FORTY-SEVENTH
SEASON
1946-47

SATURDAY, 19th APRIL, 1947, at 6-30.

Philharmonic Hall.

MESSIAH

LIVERPOOL WELSH CHORAL UNION
Chorus-Master: Dr. CALEB E. JARVIS

LIVERPOOL PHILHARMONIC ORCHESTRA
Leader: DAVID WISE

SOLOISTS:
ISOBEL BAILLIE
KATHLEEN FERRIER
PETER PEARS
HAROLD WILLIAMS

CONDUCTOR:
Dr. MALCOLM SARGENT

PROGRAMME   SIXPENCE

Programme of the wonderful concert attended by Horst Alexander in 1947

*Horst, Ruth, Birgitt and Jörg Alexander with Rosa
and Bill McMillan, in Bebington, in 1966*

were made from Germany to England and from England to Germany. In 1964 Horst returned to Bebington, with his wife Ruth and children Jörg and Birgitt aged eight and four, to stay with Bill and Rosa McMillan. He was puzzled to see rooms that he had not known existed, although he had visited the house many times as a POW. Seeing Horst's bewilderment, his friends explained that in one room there had been an air-raid shelter made from heavy steel sheets. During the war a German bomb had exploded by a wall in the back garden resulting in the demolition of six ceilings in the house. Horst comments, "I cannot count how many times I have been to their house as POW – and at wintertime I was still wearing my blue uniform coat of the German air force – but never during all that time a word was mentioned about the damage caused by that bomb nor the existence of this air-raid shelter."

Horst Alexander's captivity in Britain was filled with an experience he can never forget. The fellowship with his friends in Bebington lasted more than 40 years and spread to his children. Now those English friends have passed away, but their legacy can still be felt. All the members of Herr Alexander's family, including his grandchildren, are active members of the Open Brethren in Germany, and he can look back on over 50 years of fellowship within the movement. He now knows there was a reason why he had to become a prisoner of war in England. It gave him a new life.

5. The Toolbox

The very harsh winter of the first months of 1947 was over, and at last road conditions were good. Noah Hine of Oldham, Lancashire, was driving his three-ton Bedford Luton van along Ashton New Road when it broke down. He got out and put the bonnet up, wondering what to do. After a short time a Humber Super Snipe Estate drew up behind him, and out jumped a young man who asked in a foreign accent what was wrong. "It won't start", replied Noah. The foreigner put his head under the bonnet for a couple of seconds only and said, "Go and start it." The engine immediately sprang to life. Noah was flabbergasted! Then the foreigner produced four half-pound packets of butter from the vehicle he was driving and offered them to Noah. In this time of rationing, such a gift was like gold.

Noah discovered that the helpful foreigner was a prisoner from the local POW camp. He had been to Ashton to collect supplies for the officers' mess and, it seems, had been given more butter than was expected. In addition he was mechanically minded. He had seen that the high tension lead from the middle of the distributor had come loose. All that was needed was to push it back into place.

"You must come to visit us," said Noah, and before long the offer of hospitality was accepted. The helpful prisoner was Stefan Bolz, and he brought his friend Franz Weitmann, both born in Yugoslavia though of German descent. They were welcomed by Noah, his wife Agnes and their two teenage children, Dorothy and Jeffrey. The prisoners started to visit on a regular basis, usually on Sundays. Agnes would provide a wholesome Lancashire meal as far as the rationing restrictions allowed. Occasionally tripe was served, and it was not unknown for Agnes to make a horse-meat stew. The tripe did not appeal to Stefan, and when no one was looking he put it in his pocket!

After the meal they would all sit together listening to records, playing the piano and talking. Stefan could play the violin, and Jeffrey was a good singer. Stefan and Franz were keen to improve their English and advance themselves. Franz was a professional craftsman, a cabinet maker and French polisher. He made beautifully shaped boxes, wooden sewing baskets and even a radiogram. He would sit for hours polishing his latest creation. Stefan had quite different skills, but more of him in a later story.

Jeffrey had turned 14, and later in the year he left school. He got a job

Jeffrey Hine in his garage with the tool box made by Franz Weitmann in 1947. Jeffrey, now retired, is working on his 47-year-old Jaguar XK120 Sports car ready for the spring.

as an apprentice fitter at Wren Mill in Chadderton. On hearing about Jeffrey's new job, Franz set himself another task. He started to make a tool box as a useful gift for the young man. After much careful and loving work the result was a perfectly crafted box with four drawers, a hinged section at the front and a handle. It was hand sawn and planed, with hand-made dovetails, and of course well polished (see colour photographs). This turned out to be a very strong, durable and useful possession, so indispensable in fact that it is still in use in Jeffrey's garage fifty-three years later.

6. The Man who Found a New Family and a New Way of Life

Helmut Eckardt was an only child, a rather shy young boy who lived in the very small village of Katherinenrieth near Sangerhausen, south of the Harz mountains. In 1936 at the age of 11 he was sent north to a boarding school in Barby near Magdeburg. After the initial shock of leaving his home village he became accustomed to the disciplined life of a German boarding school and the Hitler Youth movement. On leaving school in 1942 he went immediately into the German army. Early in 1945 at the age of 19, he was captured by the enemy at a crossing over the River Rhine. Thus, all his teenage years had been spent within a highly structured framework.

A New Adventure
Although he did not realise it at the time, Helmut was starting a new adventure when he became a prisoner of war. He was to discover a new country and a completely different outlook on life. After six weeks in Belgium he arrived in England with only two possessions: an aluminium horse comb and a handkerchief. Having found the horse comb somewhere he realised it was worth keeping as it would be unlikely to break. The handkerchief had once been white with a design of little squares along the edge. The first thing he remembers about arriving in England is being ordered to take a cold shower without soap or a towel. He tried to dry himself with the handkerchief and then used the comb on his hair. At his first POW camp in England, subsistence rations included rice pudding with sultanas, something he has liked ever since.

It was in Cornwall that his adventures really began. He and his fellow prisoners arrived at the railway station at the bottom of the hill in Launceston, on an exceptionally hot summer day. Laden with all the kit acquired by this time, including a heavy overcoat, they had to walk up the hill to the camp in the heat of the day. The camp consisted only of an open field, one small hut and a pile of army bell tents. If the men wanted to sleep under cover that night they had to erect a tent. One of the men was "blessed with fourth sight", as Helmut puts it. He foresaw that if the weather changed they could get wet through the skin of the tent. Therefore his group erected two tents, one inside the other. Their new home remained waterproof throughout the winter, and the doubling of the tent was never discovered.

A New Way of Life

The men were employed on Cornish farms, Helmut and two other men being billeted on a farm near Camelford, 12 miles from the camp. It was here that Helmut was to be awakened to a new way of living and thinking. The farm was run by a Mrs Mary Whitehouse, whose husband was in Germany with the British army, and whose children were away at boarding school. There were hundreds of animals on the farm, sheep, cows and horses, in fact more horses and shire ponies than cows, as Mrs Whitehouse was a keen hunter. She came from a wealthy family, her mother having been dressmaker to Queen Mary. Helmut was amazed to find that Mrs Whitehouse behaved as though rules and regulations did not exist. As he expressed it, "She did exactly as she fancied." To him, brought up under the discipline of Germany in the 1930s, boarding school life and the German army, Mrs Whitehouse seemed very unconventional and even shocking. Although she had agreed to have the three men billeted on the farm, she told them from the start she would not cook for them. They had to sleep in the saddle room of the stables and live off the land finding their own food. They learnt to make good use of a shotgun and existed mainly on rabbit, pheasant, milk and eggs.

Other than the milk round, which was done by two land girls, all the rest of the day-to-day farm work was in the hands of the three men. Helmut's responsibility was to look after the cows and sheep, quite a different life from anything he had known in Germany, but he grew to like it. He learned to ride a pony, joined the Young Farmers' Club in Camelford and had a very enjoyable time. Mrs Whitehouse did not bother to maintain her hedges and banks, with the result that her animals were apt to escape onto her neighbours' land. For this, she was not very popular in the area. One day this rather eccentric woman suddenly decided the men needed a holiday. Without informing the POW camp, she drove them 200 miles by car to Buckinghamshire where her mother lived in a large house in spacious grounds. En route they saw Stonehenge at midnight.

Helmut Eckardt, working on Mrs Whitehouse's farm in Cornwall in 1947

A New Family

Yet another new experience was to come Helmut's way. He met a family which was to change the very focus of his life. It happened in 1947, the year when his two fellow workers were both repatriated, and Mrs Whitehouse had to find replacements. She decided to employ an English couple, Mr and Mrs Daw. On leaving the navy, Mr Spenwin Daw, known as Spen, had taken a training course in farming. With his wife (known as Beekie) and his three young children, he came to live in a cottage on the farm. As they worked together with Helmut, Spen and Beekie soon became his good friends, inviting him into the cottage for meals. This family seemed to Helmut to be as unconventional as Mrs Whitehouse was. The twin girls, Rosalind (known as Hickie because she once had very bad hiccoughs) and Alison (known as Lala), had a slightly younger brother, John, then aged three. These children all had strong personalities and, despite their young age, "played Helmut up". He had to learn how to hold his own with three spirited children, something which was to stand him in good stead a few years later.

The following year, Helmut received the good news that he was now free from his prisoner status and was permitted to return to Germany, but he had to make an important decision. Should he go home to his parents in the village of Katherinenrieth or not? By this time he had grown to appreciate the less formal way of life in Britain, so completely different from what he remembered of Germany. Just as important to his decision was the fact that he had found a new family: Spen, Beekie, Hickie, Lala and John had more or less adopted him. In particular, Helmut felt that Beekie, a very nice person, had become like a second mother to him.

He did return to Germany briefly, but only to collect his back pay and be dismissed from the army. While in Cologne, Helmut made another decision. He spent his army pay on a second-hand camera which was to become more important to him than he could have guessed at the time. Unfortunately the camera was impounded by British customs, perhaps because Helmut could not produce a receipt. After a delay of weeks, he was forced to pay for the return of the camera, but as things turned out, it was probably worth the money.

Back in Cornwall, Helmut returned to his new family, the Daws, and resumed work for Mrs Whitehouse. But one day an event took place which was to lose him his job. It was his task to clean Mrs Whitehouse's unusual car, an expensive French "La Salle" with a foldaway top, her pride and joy, but very difficult to start if wet. Helmut was in the habit of putting a hessian bag over the engine, under the bonnet, to shield it from the damp. One Saturday he forgot to remove the sacking. Then began what Helmut calls something like a French farce. When Mrs Whitehouse was out driving, the car caught fire outside the local pub.

Her three bachelor neighbours came with a lorry, offering to help. They tied the car behind the lorry to tow it home, but, perhaps because they had had some drinks in the pub, the car ended up in the ditch. As a result, despite his years of loyal work, Helmut was dismissed.

He was fortunate, however, to obtain work on another farm, near enough for him to stay in contact with his new family. But the Daws had now decided to leave Cornwall as Mrs Whitehouse was inclined to pay staff only when she felt like it. They found work on a farm 200 miles away near Heathfield in Sussex. This was a terrible blow for Helmut: he did not want to be separated from his new family, and they were reluctant to lose him. Before leaving, Spen asked him, "If there's a chance of a job on the farm in Sussex, will you come?" He was only too willing to agree. The only vacant job turned out to be a tractor driver, for which Helmut had very little experience, but, thanks to Spen, Helmut got the job and followed his new family to Sussex!

A New Career

With an increasing interest in the camera which he had paid both to obtain and then to retrieve from customs, Helmut began taking a photographic magazine. He spotted a mysterious advertisement which read, "Are you interested in travel and photography, and are you good with children?" He discovered that the job entailed taking individual photographs of schoolchildren. His energetic experiences with Hickie, Lala and John led him to feel some confidence about working with children, so he expressed an interest in the post, which he saw as a welcome change from farming. He heard nothing for several months. Then, suddenly, he was asked to go to a car park at the rear of the Odeon cinema in Slough, Berkshire. Helmut borrowed a car to travel the 70 miles from Sussex, across London, to Slough. By 4 pm it was dark, and it seemed rather a strange setting for a job interview. Two men in a large black car had a long talk with him, and one week later they rang to ask him to start the job the following week.

However, Helmut had a problem. He had no car of his own, an essential item for the new job. Neither he nor Spen had managed to save any money, but luckily a fellow farm worker generously offered to lend him £100. With three days to spare before starting his new job, Helmut bought a second-hand car with his friend's money and took up the new role with enthusiasm, only to find that his first solo assignment was a disaster. When the first school in Windsor received their photographs from the laboratory, the tops of the children's heads had been cut off! Helmut had to revisit the school and start all over again.

About this time the Daw family left Sussex and moved to Surbiton, southwest of London. Helmut of course went with them, travelling from

Surbiton to schools across the south of England. In 1952 he was offered a job at the firm's headquarters in Sturminster Newton in Dorset, and after commuting for a while he reluctantly decided he must move nearer his work. At the age of 26, therefore, he left Spen, Beekie and the children, the family which had been the cause of his staying in England. He had spent five years of his life with them, and they never lost touch.

A New Home

Lodging in the pub at Sturminster Newton, he met many colourful local residents. Among them was a retired air force officer with a handle-bar moustache who owned the old established ironmonger's shop. He was an outstanding personality and a very good artist, and later was to play the role of best man at Helmut's wedding. Helmut also met Mary Curtis who worked for the same firm, and she was the one who was to become his wife. Helmut grew to like the town where three other former German POWs also were now living.

As Helmut was an only child, his parents were disappointed he never returned to live in the village of Katherinenrieth or to the area south of the Harz mountains, which became part of the German Democratic Republic. In the late 1950s he was granted British citizenship giving him an advantage in this respect. With a British passport he could go in and out of East Germany, which as a German citizen he would not have been able to do, so from then onwards he visited his relations each year. Even after his parents died, Helmut and Mary visited the area about every three years where they still have friends.

The photographic firm closed down in 1958, but Helmut carried on taking photographs of schoolchildren on his own, visiting schools across southern England, but eventually concentrating on schools in Dorset and adjoining counties. In 1964 he and Mary were married and later managed to have new premises built in the centre of Sturminster Newton, a photographic shop with studio and a processing room, and an apartment above, in which they still live.

Helmut Eckardt, with camera, 2000

Over the years, as well as his ongoing work with school children, Mr Helmut Eckardt, the photographer, has built up his business in the town. For about two decades he had a retail shop selling photographic equipment. He attended hundreds of weddings and was well known for his studio portraits. He recorded the town's heritage and took pictures of the carnival each year from 1955 to the end of the century. Many of his photographs can still be seen in the shop, now run by his son Jonathan who has branched out into the making of commercial videos.

The war changed the course of Helmut's life completely. The freedom of the British lifestyle refreshed him, he met unconventional and interesting people, he found friendship and support when he needed it most, he acquired a new family and a second "mother". He discovered a career, married a British woman and made the south of England his new home. As he sums it all up he adds, "The war for me was not all bad, was it? I have no regrets."

7. The Wonderful Present

During the war, Sidney Taylor, a young married man, served in the National Fire Service. Although he lived in Lancashire he was seconded during the blitz to assist resident fire brigade personnel in Coventry, Plymouth and Manchester, being away from home for weeks at a time. Many other fire officers were sent similarly from various parts of Britain to the cities suffering most from German bombing raids. When he was home, one of Sidney Taylor's responsibilities was to visit the local cotton mill, which had been turned into an enormous camp for German prisoners of war. His tasks were to attend to fire safety systems and fire prevention measures and to check water storage facilities.

During one of his many visits to the mill he became friendly with a prisoner. Although there were no proper facilities for wood working, this man carved an ingenious sewing box by hand, using what pieces of wood he could find. It was of a sturdy construction with one large and four smaller sections for sewing materials, opening out in a concertina fashion, and with a central handle. The box measured one foot wide,

The sewing box made by a prisoner

six inches deep and seven inches high. The prisoner gave this unusual wooden creation to Mr Taylor as an unexpected gift for his seven-year-old daughter, Renée.

To a little girl growing up in wartime, this was a marvellous possession. Renée started to put cottons in the box, then pins, needles and scissors until it was nearly full. In fact it has been filled with sewing materials ever since and used and treasured throughout the decades. Renée's name is now Mrs Longson, but she has never known the name of the gentleman who gave her the exciting present. She feels whoever it was can be justly proud of his skills. As it was so well made, and as Renée has taken good care of it for over 50 years, the box is likely to see many more years of regular use (see colour photographs).

In the 1960s, Renée also joined the fire brigade, the first woman in her town to follow her father into the service. She was a control room operator mobilising fire appliances, but in those days women were not allowed to fight fires themselves. About this time she noticed that sewing boxes similar to hers, if somewhat larger, appeared on the commercial market. She wondered then if the gentleman who made her original box had taken out a patent on its design and gone into the wholesale market! She may never know the answer, and neither is she likely to find out the name of the kind German who took such trouble to make her special box. She reflects that, "Even when our countries were at war, during those terrible years, people were still able to show kindnesses to each other." In her case it was a kindness she is never likely to forget.

8. It's Never Too Late

Ernst Siebels on leave in 1944. Left to right: his elder brother, himself, his mother, his father and a nephew

In the year 2000, Herr Ernst Siebels was a happily retired business man living with his wife Christa in the small town of Meppen in northwest Germany near the Dutch border. He had, however, one regret. He felt he had not properly said 'thank you' to people who had shown him kindness at a crucial stage in his life over 50 years before.

In his late teenage years, while thousands of his peers were fighting in northern Europe or living in prison camps in USA or Britain, Ernst had found himself in the Mediterranean, but not on holiday! The German naval ship on which he was manning anti-aircraft guns was sunk north of the island of Crete. Ernst and other members of the crew escaped onto the small volcanic island of Santorini in the Aegean Sea. There they took over the duties of the German garrison stationed on the island. At one point they captured nine British sailors when a small British sailing ship sank after attacking a larger German merchant ship in the harbour. After several weeks, however, the men of both sides were picked up by a British warship, the Ajax, and the Germans were taken as prisoners of war to Egypt. First they were in Alexandria and then Port Said, before arriving at a

Ernst Siebels and two comrades manning anti-aircraft guns on the ship Seeräuber at Piraeus, Athens in May 1944

large POW camp in Ismailia where Ernst was kept for two years until after the end of the war. For all this time the men lived in tents and slept in hollows dug into the sand.

At this camp, and at Ernst's next camp in Benghazi on the coast of Lybia, he was given the chance to attend classes to improve his general education. He was very pleased to take up all these

Ernst Siebels as a POW in Lybia in the summer of 1947

opportunities because he had left school at the age of 14, spending the following three years learning to be a bank clerk before volunteering for the German navy. In the camp's classes he chose to specialise in the English language and European history.

One day he was asked if he would like to go to England to take part in a "re-education programme". This was the British government's attempt to influence the attitudes of Germans away from Hitler's National Socialism and towards democracy. With his growing interest in the English language, Ernst jumped at the suggestion. Joining fifteen other prisoners in Port Said, he was put on a large British ship carrying troops home to Liverpool via Malta. On board, the Germans were not treated as prisoners or enemies, but were allowed to have meals with the British troops, none of whom showed any objection. Ernst was impressed by this egalitarian treatment.

It was July 1947 when he arrived in England. After three years in the desert, he found it a pleasure to see stone houses, gardens and trees. By this time, many restrictions on prisoners in Britain had been lifted. Ernst remembers going into the town, seeing pictures at the cinema and standing up while "God save the King" was sung. It seemed to him that people did not care whether he was a prisoner or not, and "amongst them all were the lovely, smiling girls of my age! I felt like a guest in England and not any more a POW. I could hardly imagine that they had been my enemy".

This attitude was reinforced by the courses at Wilton Park Camp in Beaconsfield, Buckinghamshire, the Training Centre for the re-education programme. There were about 100 students on Ernst's course, half from POW camps in Britain and most of the rest civilians from Germany. Years later, Ernst discovered that among the German civilians present on his course had been men such as Rudolf Augstein, the founder of the weekly news magazine *Der Spiegel*, and Rainer Barzel, who became President of the German parliament, as well as former members of the hand-picked so-called "SS Panzer Division Leibstandarte", meaning "bodyguards".

Into this five-week course were packed many lectures and discussions, including topics such as political life in England, the development of Great Britain as a social and political unit, and problems of democracy; German history 1870-1918, the Weimar republic, from Weimar to Hitler, and the history of the Third Reich; also, the individual and the state, comparative democracies, problems of world hunger, international relations and world politics.

A tutor was assigned to groups of six or eight students to help them to assimilate the information and ideas. All discussions were conducted in a spirit of openness, and the students experienced the power of dialogue. They were taken by their tutors to see coal mines and factories. They visited London, the seat of democratic government and saw parliament in action. Ernst felt that his mind was being opened, and he was suddenly able to see everything with a new perspective. He is now certain that his life would have gone in quite a different direction but for this episode. He still has the lectures in a drawer, and many, many times over the years he has taken them out and re-read them. His experiences at Wilton Park Camp meant that, later in life, he was keen that his four children should each have a good academic education. Even though he and his wife found it quite hard to find the finance, they are very proud that all obtained university degrees.

Following this five-week period Ernst was sent to Norton Camp, near Mansfield in Nottinghamshire, which was known as "the University behind barbed wire". It was run by the YMCA with the support of the war office, enabling men to take their studies further, especially if their university education had been interrupted by the war. However, by joint agreement, the leader of the camp and Ernst decided that he would not benefit from further prolonged study, and so he left, having already received plenty of new ideas for the moment!

Group from Wilton Park Course visiting London, Sept 1947. Tutor in front middle. Ernst Siebels second from right

It was in the northeast of England, however, that Ernst was shown most kindness as a prisoner of war. Over 50 years later, when he was 75, this was the period in his life for which he still felt regret. He had arrived at Wolviston Hall north of Stockton-on-Tees, at the end of October 1947. Every week, the prisoners whose names were listed on a blackboard left this camp to go home to Germany. Although Ernst guessed that his turn would not come until the next spring at the earliest, he never let a day pass without looking at the board, longing for the moment when he could start the journey home. He passed the time by attending as many of the seminars provided for prisoners as possible. He also

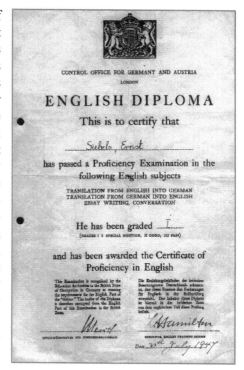

Examinations taken in Cambridge, July 1947

found work whenever he could such as in sugar beet fields, with a coal dealer, in a cement factory and doing private gardening. With the money he earned he bought coffee, tea and sugar to send home to Germany where such items were in very scarce supply.

One day, when Ernst had been without work for some days, a comrade asked him to help to unload lorries, for which they were paid by the hour. In this way Ernst became friendly with this man who had been in the camp for years, during which time he had made friends with an English family. Then came the time when the man was listed on the blackboard to be sent home. His English friends, sad to see him go, asked if he could introduce them to another prisoner to take his place. He chose Ernst. On the following Saturday, Ernst was taken and introduced to the man of the house, Charlie, his wife Beatrice and their four children aged between 6 and 20. The fifth was away in the army. Because it was the last visit of the original prisoner, the whole family was present and additional friends too, making a large group. This was the first time Ernst had been accepted as a guest in an English family, and indeed the first time he had been in a private home of any kind for some years. He enjoyed the experience so much he could not hide his happiness.

When it was time to leave, the atmosphere was full of emotion as the family bade farewell to the prisoner about to be repatriated. Even Charlie, the man of the house, had tears in his eyes. When Ernst was leaving, he thanked them for a lovely day, and Beatrice invited him very earnestly to come regularly to their house whenever he could. Beatrice was keen to befriend prisoners, hoping that if her son, now away in the army, were to be in a difficult situation in a foreign land someone would help him likewise.

Ernst visited his new friends three or four times every week from then onwards, during the three month period from 7 December 1947 to the beginning of March 1948 when he was suddenly released. He recalls, "Charlie showed me his town with its old churches and other remarkable buildings, and I noted how proud he was of his town. We went to football matches at the weekend and to the club where Charlie was a member. We filled out the football coupons, getting hot heads, and marked the crosses at the favourite names of the teams on the sheet, but we never won even a penny! I never before had heard of this kind of betting!" The town shown with such pride was Stockton, and the club was the working men's club in the neighbouring village of Norton.

As the end of the year drew near, Ernst was delighted to have a family to be with at Christmas, the first time for six years. He thought of his own family in Meppen which had suffered shelling during the war. As his father had died in 1945 after an operation, it was his mother to whom he wrote describing his experiences in England, and his letters were kept safely over the years by his sister. On 14 December 1947, he wrote:

It is now the 6th year I will not be at home with you at Christmas. But this time you must not be anxious. This year I am very well provided for. My 'English family' take care of me. They treat me as their own son, and do everything – as well as possible – to help me to forget being a German POW. Could you send a letter and thank them for what they are doing for your son? I am invited to spend the Christmas period in their home. And besides I am with them every second evening, having fun and pleasure with parents and children, enjoying the evening meal at the family table on arriving, just as at home. And before I leave, in addition tea and cakes! But what depresses me always again is, I only can say 'thanks', nothing more!

Ernst's letter written on 28 December carried a description of Christmas with Charlie and Beatrice.

Dear Mother,

Today I will tell you how I spent Christmas in the English family. Briefly, it was simply fantastic! On Christmas Eve, after having returned from working, I prepared myself for the visit. Took a shower, packed my luggage with the necessary travelling equip-ment. When did I last do that? At 7 o'clock I arrived at my family.

*Card Ernst sent to his mother at Christmas 1947 saying,
"To my dear Mother, Christmas 1947. With my only
wish to be with you at home by Christmas 1948"*

When I entered the room, it looked a bit strange to me, because the room was beautifully decorated, but with a lot of colour, like we do at home when there is a birthday to be celebrated. But I got used to it, the longer I was there. We spent the evening in singing English and German carols, and I told them what we do at home to celebrate Christmas Eve. The candles on the Christmas tree here in England, for example, are lit on Christmas morning (or not at all) instead of on Christmas Eve, as we do. Of course I remember my last Christmas at home, it was 1941, 6 years ago! You wouldn't believe, dear mother, how I do enjoy the time with these people. They are so joyful and friendly, and, as I told you before, treat me as their own son! At 2 o'clock we finally went to bed. For the first time since the 25.2.1944 a real bed was waiting for me! [That was the last day of his final two weeks' leave before being captured.] The parents had given their own one to me and slept in the living room. I could not fall asleep for a long time. I had to think over the fact that these human beings have done so many good things for me. What a pity you couldn't have seen me. The lady is doing every thing to make my time as a prisoner absent from home as easy and pleasurable as possible and to compensate me for missing life in our family. On Christmas morning I was hardly awake when both of them came in and served, I could not believe it, tea, cakes and breakfast, such as I received not even at home, except when I was ill! Later on, the candles on the tree were lit, and we exchanged presents. From the parents I got a razor, from the daughter a notebook, and from her girlfriend a cigarette case. At that moment

my conscience pricked me, and I could hardly prevent shedding tears!
I ask you again, please write a letter to the family, thanking them for
all the good things they are doing for me. To say thanks is at present
the only thing we can do.

Before Ernst left Wolviston Hall the following March he had become
even closer to his English friends, and they to him. Without the usual
warning, though, the day came for Ernst to go by train to Harwich for
the ship home. He was not even able to inform his friends of his departure.
Then, only a few minutes before the train was due to leave the station,
although Ernst never knew how it happened, Beatrice arrived exhausted,
with her small son holding one hand and carrying several packages for
Ernst in the other hand. He will never forget that picture of her, and as
he said goodbye he could not prevent tears coming into his eyes. What
he did not know then was that he would never see Charlie and Beatrice
again. The surprise packages contained sandwiches, fruit and chocolates
which Ernst shared with some of his friends on the journey. After his
return home, for some reason no letters were exchanged, for which, as
the years went by, Ernst could not forgive himself. Neither had his
mother written to his English friends, as he had exhorted her to do: she
did not know anyone who could translate a letter for her.

* * *

The story jumps forward to Herr Siebels' retirement years. He and his
wife Christa were having a conversation over a Rotary dinner in July
1998 with an English couple, Malcolm and Joan Dennett. The English
couple were members of Sutton Nonsuch Rotary Club in Surrey, England
which is twinned with Herr Siebels' Rotary Club in Meppen, Germany.
During the meal Herr Siebels talked about his experiences in England of
50 years before, and his feelings of shame that he had never contacted
the family after his return to Germany to thank them for their kindness.
Mr Dennett offered to try to trace the family, but Herr Siebels was
doubtful about such a suggestion.

Then, eighteen months later, Malcolm Dennett saw there was to be a
documentary programme on BBC television about friendships made
between British people and German prisoners of war, and he remembered
Ernst Siebels' story. He recorded the programme and sent it to him in
Meppen. The programme was the *Timewatch* documentary, *The Germans
We Kept*, based largely on the book, *Enemies Become Friends*, written
by the present author, Pamela Howe Taylor. In the accompanying letter,
Mr Dennett repeated his previous offer to try to trace Herr Siebels'
English friends. After much thought, Herr Siebels agreed to take up this
offer. Unfortunately he could not remember the full name or address of
his erstwhile friends, only the name 'Charlie' who worked in a bicycle
repair shop and was very keen on football. He also remembered that

Ernst Siebels in September 2000 outside the house where his "English Family", Charlie and Beatrice Adams, had lived in 1947

Charlie's daughter had a friend called Maureen. It was not much for Mr Dennett to work on.

After nothing came of three or four enquiries to official organisations, Mr Dennett had the idea of contacting a Teesside newspaper to ask for their help, and Herr Siebels provided an old photograph of himself as a POW. This was published in the *Middlesbrough Evening Gazette* under the headline, "My friends in the North. Ex-POW Ernst on a mission", giving the details of Charlie, the bicycle shop and the name Maureen. On the night of publication, Tuesday 11 April 2000, Jack Adams of Norton near Stockton was reading the Gazette, not something he did every evening, when the hairs on the back of his neck stood on end. The description fitted his own family. It was a strange feeling. He had been a boy of five when his parents had become friendly with German prisoners of war. Charlie and Beatrice Adams were no longer alive, but Jack and his wife Ann lived in the same area not far from his childhood home. That same evening he telephoned the number given in the newspaper and spoke to Mr Dennett in Surrey, who was surprised and delighted to obtain the response he was hoping for, and at such speed.

Thus began communication between Herr Siebels and Mr Adams, and Jack Adams invited Ernst to visit them in England. Five months later Ernst made the journey to see Jack and Ann Adams in the northeast. He met their three sons and five grandchildren and saw some of the places he remembered from the past, in particular the outside of the house where his "English family" had lived, which seemed to have changed very little over the years. He was taken to a busy working men's club, "Malleable Club" in Norton, possibly the same one he visited with Charlie but now rebuilt in new premises. There he met many friendly people, including one whose son was living in Berlin. He was introduced to another former resident of the camp at Wolviston, German ex-air force pilot and now Rotary member, Bill Predegar, who had married an English woman and settled in the area.

During this visit Ernst felt sad that he had not tried to find his "English family" years before. However, he was deeply grateful for the opportunity he now had to express his appreciation to Charlie and Beatrice's children and grandchildren for the friendship he had received. He sent a message of thanks to the Gazette saying,

Although it has taken me 53 years to find my family in the northeast I've never forgotten them and their kindness. I have remembered them every Christmas. They taught me to believe in the generosity of people who had every reason to hate me.

The following May, Jack and Ann Adams and their 13-year-old granddaughter Sophie paid a three day visit to Meppen where Ernst and Christa Siebels made them very welcome. This was their first visit to Germany, and for Ann and Sophie their first ever air flight. Ernst showed his visitors the original letters he sent home from England in his POW days, which his sister had kept safely. They looked at old photographs and compared life in Germany with life in England.

Excitement was added to this visit by several unusual sightseeing outings, such as a trip to see the new Trans-Rapid Magnet hover train, due to be delivered to China in two months' time (where Sophie was allowed to sit in the driver's seat), and a visit to the biggest shipbuilding yard in Germany, which builds 90,000-ton ships although it is situated 30 miles inland.

They were taken also to see a peat bog and factory where Ernst had worked for 43 years, rising from book-keeper in 1952 to Chief Executive Officer of the Klasmann Group before his retirement in 1989. When the Group joined with another company to become the Klasman-Deilmann

Jack, Sophie and Ann Adams with Christa Siebels in Herr and Frau Siebels' home in Meppen, Germany in May 2001

Company, Ernst was asked to be Chairman of the Supervisory Board until 1995 when his younger son Dr Norbert Siebels became one of the two Directors. Norbert gave Jack, Ann and Sophie a conducted tour of the site which encompasses a 15,000-acre peat bog on Bourtanger Moor, a peat regeneration area almost as large, and a modern factory to treat and pack peat and associated products for the agricultural and horticultural industries. On their tour they saw 10,000-year-old peat being excavated and ancient tree roots, as well as some of the factory processes, ending with a film in the offices and a refreshing cup of tea.

Jack, Ann and Sophie felt very welcome in Germany and thoroughly enjoyed these unusual experiences. Unfortunately there was not time to do everything in three days. Meeting other members of Ernst and Christa's family (four children and twelve grandchildren) has to wait for a future visit.

Although Jack is not old enough to remember much about the mid-1940s, he is very glad that the link has been renewed with his family. He feels quite proud of his parents but comments that "in those days, when most people had very little, they offered their help and kindness not for reward but simply to help a fellow human being through a difficult time". Since the link has been renewed Jack has talked to many people about friendship with German prisoners. He has found that most people hold no bitterness towards German people despite two world wars. "On the contrary," he says, "they hold them in high esteem." Jack's own philosophy is summed up by the phrase, "Live and let live."

Malcolm Dennett of Surrey is satisfied that, by means of modern communications and with the aid of the press, he has been able to help a German fellow member of Rotary International. "We have", he says, "a happy conclusion to a story about international friendship which lies at the heart of the Rotary movement".

Readers may wonder why Ernst never made an effort to contact Charlie and Beatrice while they were alive. In fact, every Christmas he was ashamed when he remembered the wonderful hospitality of Christmas 1947. Now things are different. He is convinced that his decision to agree to his Rotary friend's suggestion to trace the family was entirely right. He is so joyful with the result of the belated search that he does not much care what other people may think about the 50 year delay. Now he faces Christmas with equanimity and a deep satisfaction in knowing Jack, Ann, their children and grandchildren, his "English family". Herr Siebels harboured his regret for rather more years than expected, but in the end he found it was never too late to say "Thank you".

9. A Real Gentleman

One day in the early 1980s Peter and Molly Spencer were sitting on a bench waiting for a bus in Kettering Road, Northampton. Sharing the bench with them was a smart gentleman dressed in a blue suit and highly polished black shoes. He also had a broad smile. They got talking together and promised to meet again.

The man's name was Frank Mansfield-Smith, and he was in his late 60s. When Peter Spencer called on him on his way home from work one day, he found him busy in his large garden. He lived alone in a detached bungalow called "Chypraze" at Threeways in Moulton on the northern outskirts of Northampton. Peter began calling in to have a chat with Frank on a regular basis, and Frank would set aside his garden tools, brew the tea and usually produce some doughnuts. Peter was soon aware that Frank kept the bungalow and garden in immaculate condition. To keep him company, he had a pair of finches in his conservatory. He loved music, listening each week to *Friday Night is Music Night* on the wireless, but he had no wish to own a television. Over the coming months, as the friendship developed, Frank told Peter and Molly how he came to be living in Moulton and in the bungalow with the strange name, "Chypraze".

Frank was born Franz August Bytomski on 20 August 1912 in Paulsdorf in Hindenburg in the south east of Germany, a town now in the south of Poland and renamed Zabrze. After working in his grandparents' hardware shop, he was called up into the German army and sent to fight in Russia. He was shot and wounded in Stalingrad, and taken back to Germany for treatment. Some of his comrades were frozen to death where they stood in the icy Russian weather, so Franz believed his wounds had saved his life. In June 1944 at the age of 31, he was captured in Caen, Normandy and sent to England, first to a POW camp in Norwich and then to Boughton Camp near Moulton in Northampton.

Frank went on to tell Peter and Molly the unusual story of how two ladies became his friends and benefactors. Miss Caroline Smith of Moulton had been a nursing Sister in the First World War. Just before Christmas 1947 she wrote to Boughton Camp to ask if two prisoners would like to spend Christmas Day with her and her older sister, Mrs Lack. This was how Franz and a comrade met the two ladies who were then aged 61 and 71. Being given an extremely warm welcome, the prisoners were very impressed with how lovely the bungalow was with its garden. The dining room table was laid out for the delicious Christmas dinner, and Franz tasted roast turkey for the first time, as

The site of Boughton Camp as it looked in 1998

in Germany the usual Christmas fare was goose. Both sisters played the piano, Franz sang Christmas carols in German, the other prisoner played the violin, and they all had a very happy Christmas Day together.

From that time onwards a friendship developed between Franz and the two sisters, to such an extent that he began looking after their garden and then undertaking some of the maintenance in the bungalow, such as painting and decorating. When the time came for Franz to be repatriated in mid-1948, he chose to stay in Northampton as by then he had a job on a farm opposite the bungalow. The sisters offered him accommodation in "Chypraze", and he became almost like a member of the family.

Franz had great difficulty tracing any of his own relatives. The town of his birth had become part of Poland and his eldest brother's family had left their home in the east of Germany in 1945, to flee west along with thousands of others who were afraid of the Russians. In 1956 Franz returned to Germany to seek his relations, staying for a time with the director of an organisation which helped former prisoners of war. Eventually he found his oldest brother, almost 20 years his senior: he and his wife were then living near Düsseldorf. Franz also saw his sister and his brother's eldest daughter, Ursula Klein. Although he was happy to have renewed contact with members of his family, he never had any intention of staying in Germany or Poland. He returned to England where he felt at home and was very happy living with the two sisters, though unfortunately the older sister, Mrs Lack, died that same year at the age of 80.

In the mid 1960s Franz was delighted that his brother and sister-in-law were able to visit him in England and meet Miss Smith, whom they addressed as "Auntie Caroline". In 1965 Franz decided to change his name to a more English sounding one: from Franz August Bytomski he

Franz Bytomski and his brother and sister-in-law with Miss Caroline Smith in her garden in the mid-1960s

officially became Frank Augustus Mansfield-Smith. His mother's maiden name had been "Mansfeld", and "Smith" was, of course, in honour of his great friend Miss Caroline Smith.

Besides working on the farm, he had two other jobs over the years, first in a factory in Towcester ten miles south of Northampton, and then working for a paint retailer in Northampton itself. For more than 20 years he and Miss Smith lived under the same roof, and he found himself in the position of looking after her more and more as she became older. By the time she was 90 she was bedridden, and Frank was on call day and night, undertaking cheerfully all the tasks which fell to him.

At Christmas 1977 Frank wrote a letter to a local newspaper, recalling the Christmas of 30 years before when he had first met Miss Caroline Smith. He concluded the letter with these words:

Miss Smith, a retired nursing Sister, is now 91 and bedridden. The nurses call every day giving her a good wash. I take care of her day and night and look after the home. Miss Smith is a very nice person and a dear friend to me, and I thank God every day for having her still with me to celebrate this Christmas festival as well, happily together.

Not long after this Miss Smith passed away. The bungalow, with its conservatory and beautiful garden, was left to Frank, and he continued to look after it with the utmost care and attention to detail, sharing it with his pair of finches and any friends who called to see him such as the new friends he had met at the bus stop, Peter and Molly Spencer (see colour photographs).

As Christmas was always a special time for Frank with his happy memories, he was pleased to receive invitations to visit neighbours and friends on that day each year. At Christmas 1987, to mark the 40th anniversary of that all-important first Christmas, Frank wrote these words,

> I love my new country, my home and the English way of life, but I miss my dear friend the late Miss Caroline Smith, ex-nursing Sister, very very much. My happy Christmas memories will still be with her, till we meet.

Frank Mansfield-Smith with Molly and Peter Spencer in their garden in September 1992, four months before Frank's death

Frank kept in contact with his remaining relatives in Germany. When his brother and sister-in-law died, their daughter, Ursula Klein, maintained the correspondence with her "Uncle Gustel". In 1990 she and her husband, Herbert, drove to England to see him. Although they did not really know each other, they all had a lovely time together visiting Cambridge, Stratford-upon-Avon and of course Northampton and Frank's inherited home in Moulton. Ursula thought highly of the two ladies who had "given this young homeless man a place in their life".

Frank often visited Peter and Molly in their home and became a good friend of the family. They described him as "a real gentleman". It was a sad day for them when Frank died in January 1993 at the age of 80, having had heart trouble for nearly ten years. He had written to a friend in Germany at the beginning of the month that he was looking forward to the spring to do some gardening. Frank Augustus Mansfield-Smith was buried in Moulton, the village which had changed his life and become his home for nearly 50 years, thanks to the unexpected friendship offered to a prisoner of war by two elderly sisters.

10. The Baker's Story

Harold Hall, born in Nuneaton, Warwickshire, in 1908, was a baker. During the war he stood outside the bake-house very early in the morning watching wave after wave of bombers flying towards the east coast of England to rain destruction on Dresden, Hamburg and other German cities. When bread rationing began he said it was a farce. There was not a shortage of bread: the problem was quality not quantity. The flour he and other bakers had to use was made from wheat which must have begun re-sprouting. The flour clung to the baker's hands and set like cement. The resulting loaf, when cut, looked and tasted like cardboard.

One day in 1946, Harold was cycling up the Cock and Bear Hill in Nuneaton when a convoy passed him, lorries full of German prisoners. They were going to an ex-army camp in the grounds of Arbury Hall, just south of Nuneaton, having recently arrived from prison camps in Canada and USA. As the last lorry struggled over the hill, a woman rushed into the road spitting after it. Harold realised that the hatred engendered by the war was still intense, but he believed there was only one alternative to hatred – love and friendship. He and his wife Lilian talked this over, and when they noticed prisoners being allowed out of the camp, they decided to take some positive action.

They found out that prisoners could visit a private home, if the hosts had written to the commandant asking for permission on their behalf. It was January 1947 when Harold and Lilian sent their letter to Arbury Hall Camp, and as a result two men came to their home one Saturday afternoon. One of them was in charge of the camp postal service and could speak English fairly well. His name was Karl Schuchardt, and his friend was Gerard Winkler. They met Harold and Lilian and their four children, Shirley aged 12, Derris aged 10, David aged 7 and Lesley aged 3. With Karl translating, they all talked together as best they could and then sat down to tea, which included fresh bread, of course. It was a hurried affair, as the hosts had not realised the prisoners had to be back in camp by dark which was about 4:30 pm at that time of year. Nevertheless, it was the start of a friendship, and the two men returned to the Hall family each week. This arrangement did not last long, though, as these two prisoners were among the first to be repatriated. Harold and Lilian had never been out of Britain. Little did they know that the next time they would see Karl and Gerard would be in another country and in very different circumstances.

Before the two men left the camp they introduced two more prisoners, Robert Groll and Matthias Schwalb. Robert Groll, from a small town north of Cologne, perfected his game of darts on his many visits to the Hall family and probably beat Harold more times than he lost. Matthias Schwalb was about 20 years of age, having been drafted into the army on leaving school and sent to Jersey as part of the German occupation of the Channel Islands. He was a bright young man who showed all the potential for a good career ahead of him. Harold noticed that Matthias learnt English quickly, and after a short time he spoke it almost perfectly. His father had been a headmaster, demoted under Hitler, and killed by shell fire when the Allies crossed the Rhine.

But these were not the only prisoners to visit the baker's family. Many of the larger camps had a German pastor among the prisoners, and the first pastor at the Arbury Hall Camp was Max Killius. He became a regular visitor, having something in common with Harold, who was a Methodist local preacher. Max was an artist, and one of his hobbies was to paint in watercolours. Unfortunately no paints were available to the prisoners, but Max improvised using pigments from plants and flowers he found in the hedgerows. In this way he painted a wonderful picture of Arbury Hall, the eighteenth-century Gothic-style mansion, set in land-scaped gardens, where the POW camp was now situated. The novelist, George Eliot, had been born on the estate. On completing the painting,

Faded photograph showing three prisoners with the Hall family in Nuneaton in 1947. Gerard Winkler, Max Killius holding Lesley Hall, Karl Schuchardt, Harold Hall. Front: Shirley, Derris and David Hall

Max gave it to Harold and Lilian as a gesture of heartfelt gratitude for their kindness (see colour photographs). One day Max arrived very excited, with a letter. His girlfriend and her mother had managed to escape from a Russian concentration camp to their home in Baden, near Lake Constance in Switzerland. In later years, Max married her, and they returned to England to see the Hall family, with their baby named after their English friend, Harald – the German spelling of Harold. It was a very moving meeting for all concerned, made more poignant when it was learnt later that Max did not live to see his son Harald grow up. He died a few years after this visit.

The second Pastor at the camp was Hanskarl Muller, a family man from Berndorf, whose children were of similar ages to those of Harold and Lilian. Lilian corresponded with Pastor Muller's wife, Rose, who was doing her best to bring up her children alone, amidst the devastation of post-war Germany. By September 1947 there was a drought in Germany and fear that the potato harvest would be very poor. Rose explained in a letter, "That will bring to our people who had to feed almost exclusively upon potatoes in the last years the starvation, and to innumerable men, death. Those farmers who had eight cows in shed had to sell already more than half. Thereby our fat ration which was till now tiny will be cut once more because then there will be no milk and butter. We have only 100 grams of meat per week, although so many cattle are butchered day by day." Regarding clothing she explained, "We have got clothes coupons for the children, but there is no material in any shops for boys' shirts or even wool for socks or pullovers." She was fearful that her eldest boy had caught typhus, which was rife, but it turned out to be cold as a result of the thinness of his trousers. She had previously given her husband's trousers to refugees from the east who lived in their village in "bitterest misery".

The Hall family responded to this information by sending food and clothes parcels to Germany. Rose Muller wrote in January 1948 to say that the bigger of two parcels had arrived in a very damaged state, but "very wonderful were the many shoes which appeared" out of it. Also, "the good butter, what a joy! Our rations are very scarce, it is true, but fat is nearly [impossible] to get. We have to go for it often four to five times to the nearby little town, and generally they laugh there when we ask for fat. But there is no wonder after the failure of crop of the last year." The delicious jam and dried apricots were mentioned too, before the letter ended with these words, "God bless you and many heartiest thanks for all your love you do for our Hanskarl and us. Your grateful Rose". It seems that Rose came to think of Lilian almost as a sister, writing in one letter, "You would resemble so closely to my youngest sister who is beloved so particularly by all of us."

The third and last Pastor at the camp was Dr Arthur Leckscheidt, a Lutheran who had survived the last days of the war in Berlin. Dr Leckscheidt, a musician with the Berlin Philharmonic Orchestra, had apparently volunteered to come to England and change places with Pastor Muller, who then returned home to his wife and family. Many years later, Harold read in a book about the fall of Berlin, that this same Pastor Leckscheidt had shown exceptional bravery. When the Russian bombing of the city was at its height, people heard organ music. It was Dr Leckscheidt playing the tune to Psalm 130, "Out of the depths have I cried to thee", while his church was in flames. There were stories too of how he had braved the bombing to look after Berliners and bury their dead. After his repatriation he wrote every Christmas and Easter to the Hall family until his death.

All the German prisoners who met the Hall family became great friends, and, as Harold put it years later, "they enriched our lives immeasurably. Their friendship certainly proved the panacea for all the hatred that came from other quarters." Sadly, these feelings of enrichment were quite beyond the understanding of some of the baker's acquaintances, who then gave him the cold shoulder. But the worst experience was when two prisoners accompanied the family to the Sunday School Anniversary services at the church they attended. The visiting preacher for the day turned his back on the prisoners, refusing to greet them or shake them by the hand.

Fortunately there were many people who longed for a time when everyone would work together to create a war-free Europe and a better world. Some of them decided to form a small group to learn German, but how could they find a teacher? A member of the Warwickshire Education Committee came to see Harold to ask if he thought one of the prisoners could take on the job. Harold had little hesitation in recommending the youngest prisoner, Matthias Schwalb, who had learned English so quickly and could already speak it well. Despite the fact that it was not possible for him to be paid, Matthias agreed to take on the task, perhaps remembering the teaching example of his late father. After a few months, representation was made to the War Office, and they agreed he could receive the usual night-school payments. It was quite a windfall for the young man.

The class met at the night-school premises on the corner of Coton Road and Riversley Road in Nuneaton, and the room was always full. Matthias was a good teacher and made a number of friends. Perhaps because he was one of the last soldiers to be taken prisoner in Jersey at the end of the war, he was among the last to be sent home. His long wait paid off. Just before he left, the German currency was devalued and a new currency introduced. The army pay to which he was entitled on repatriation was paid in the new currency, and that enabled him to go to university as he had intended before his father was killed. It was while

Matthias was in Nuneaton that Mrs Lilian Hall gave birth to her fifth child, Susan, in April 1948. Matthias became her godfather.

At the beginning of July, Matthias was very excited to be going home after six and a half years away. Although he was keen to go back to Germany he was also reluctant to leave his new friends. "You are partly to blame," he wrote the day before embarkation, "all of you, for making me so much at home with you. If somebody had told me two years ago that it would be so hard to leave England behind, I would have advised him to see a doctor." He concluded, "I thank you all, even the littlest one, for the nice time I had with you. God bless you all, and if there can be any more real happiness in this world, I wish it you with all my heart. Yours with love, Matt."

He sent another closely written letter to the Hall family when he arrived at the transit camp in Münster, having spent a bad crossing on heaving seas on the *Biarritz*, a 2330-ton passenger steamer from Harwich to Hook of Holland, with 800 other soldiers. On arriving in Germany after an eighteen-hour train journey, they had been met by cheering crowds of children with flowers. "The reception looked as though we had won the war," he wrote, "waving, cheering and flowers. That was our come back to Germany." Even so, "the joy of being home did not make us blind. Most of the children were poorly dressed, many of them bare footed on this cold rainy morning." Another bleak aspect of this long journey home was meeting men who had been prisoners in Russia. "Those men are broken in body and soul. Till late in the night they kept telling us, after overcoming a sort of shyness. What they tell is really dreadful and incredible, though the look of them is the best proof and wants no more words. And the strangest: they tell that Russian civilians are not treated much better. They just earn enough to buy their bread and wear the same clothes every day for years."

Of all the prisoners, he, Matthias Schwalb, was the one who kept in closest touch with the Hall family. In 1950 he returned to Nuneaton during his university vacation and stayed with them for a week. To see this talented young man, now a university student, as a free person and an equal, was a joyful experience. Harold never forgot the wonderful reunion, saying, "I always believed that peace on earth was not simply a benediction bestowed on us by God, nor a signed agreement between representatives of Governments, but a friendship forged between ordinary people. When Matt returned I knew I was right. We were delighted to see him." At that time Harold was working at Reddy's Bakery in Foleshill, eight miles south of Nuneaton, in the northern outskirts of Coventry. During Matthias's stay he wanted to visit friends in Coventry so Harold took him one morning on the back of his motorbike as far as his workplace in Foleshill, from where Matthias would make his way into Coventry. When they started out on the journey, Matthias, a keen photographer, had with him a very good Leica camera, but when they arrived the camera had gone. Harold had not time to retrace the journey as he was due at work, but at home that evening he promised to advertise for the camera in the local newspaper, thinking it was a hopeless task but worth the small expense. Two days later someone turned up with the camera. Matthias was absolutely stunned, and as Harold said, "That incident did a lot of good for national ego!"

In 1957 the Hall family had a visit from the very first prisoner they had met, Karl Schuchardt, the one who had been in charge of the camp postal service. He arrived with Else his wife and Lisalotte (Lilo for short) his secretary. He looked very different from his appearance when a prisoner in a khaki outfit with a large circle on his back. Now he was smartly dressed and drove a new Opel car. He was back in his old job at Ada-Ada (meaning "ta-ta"), the specialists in children's and ladies' shoes. The first place on his visiting list, after Arbury Hall, was Rugby where he showed Else and Lilo the actual paving slabs he had laid when he and others were taken from the camp by lorry each morning to help build streets and houses.

Harold was working at the Co-op confectionery bakery in Queen's Road, Nuneaton, when another former prisoners, Pastor Hanskarl Muller, returned to visit the family, en route to a church conference in the north of

England. It was then that Harold and Lilian decided it was about time they returned some of these visits, but Harold had sold his Ford Eight and was back to a push bike, thinking, with a growing family, he would not be able to afford another car. Fortunately the bakery stores-keeper had a neighbour with an old Austin Ten to sell. It was a 1936 model, which had been out of use since before the end of the war and still had the white paint on the wings, compulsory during wartime. Harold bought it for £22, though the engine then had to be reconditioned.

On their first ever trip abroad in 1958, Harold and Lilian with two of their children, Lesley and Susan, aged 14 and 10, and camping equip-ment, found themselves driving late

Matthias Schwalb and Harold Hall outside Cologne Cathedral in September 1958

into the night. Just before reaching Cologne they stopped for a few hours' sleep in a field and then drove on to find the little village of Alfter outside Bonn where Matthias Schwalb lived with his mother. It was five o'clock on a Sunday morning: Harold gave a little hoot and woke up the whole village. Matthias' mother, a gracious lady, received them all with real affection. An hour later the English guests were tucked up in proper beds. On waking late, they were utterly surprised to find that four former prisoners were there to meet them. They were the very first four who had come to their home in Nuneaton, Karl Schuchardt and his wife, Gerard Winkler, Robert Groll and his wife and daughter, and of course Matthias Schwalb and his mother, in whose house they were. What a reception! A trip down the Rhine was arranged and a reunion dinner at a hotel. When one of the meals arrived they all laughed out loud: sausage had been ordered, and it stretched right across the plate overhanging the edges!

The family also visited Robert Groll's home northeast of Cologne, meeting his brother and his parents, and being taken into the countryside to see two farms. The girls were fascinated by the cows and their newborn calves in what seemed to be an almost spotless cow shed. Harold and Lilian were surprised to see that the farmer had his own office with telephones and typewriter, which seemed to them, in those days, like a city firm.

In later years, the baker and his family made many more excursions to Germany. They visited Pastor Muller and his wife Rose in Ingolstadt; Else Schuchardt, Karl's widow, near Frankfurt-am-Main; Lilo, Karl's former

Matthias Schwalb, Lilian and Harold Hall at the Halls'
home in Coates near Peterborough in 1995

secretary, near Württemberg; and of course, their closest German friends Matthias Schwalb and his wife Renate and their children, Michael, Christoph, Johannes and Irene. Matthias eventually became a judge and spent his working years in the court in Cologne. On one such visit, Harold and Lilian were shown the schoolhouse where Matthias lived as a boy and from which the family had been ejected in Hitler's time. Matthias proudly posed for a photograph by the street sign, Schwalbstrasse, (meaning Swallow Street), named after, and dedicated by neighbours to, the memory of his father, the headmaster, Herr Schwalb.

Sad to say, Harold and Lilian Hall are no longer alive, but the next generation of English and Germans have kept in touch with each other across the years and the miles. David Hall reports on a visit in 1996 from Matthias's son, Christoph and his two young children. When they came to his home near Peterborough, David asked Christoph why he had brought such very young children, one only just walking and the other aged about five, on such a tiring weekend trip. Christoph replied, "I want my children to grow up knowing that there are good people in the world. Your parents were so good to my father that I want them to know such people exist."

David himself has his own memories of his childhood days, growing up with German prisoners around him. He learned to respect and admire them all. "It was, to say the least," he reflects at the age of 61, "the most educational experience of my life." Now, David proudly displays on the wall of his house a framed picture, Arbury Hall painted with plant pigments by Max Killius, a moving reminder of how the aftermath of war led to enriching friendships for the baker and his family.

11. The Talented Organist

Johannes Baumann, captured on the island of Guernsey at the age of 20, was sent to Overdale POW Camp in Skipton, West Yorkshire. He was determined to be a professional church musician, so, when conditions for prisoners became sufficiently relaxed, he asked if he could be allowed to practise on an organ somewhere. Organists in the town were approached, and Mrs Dorothy Walls responded by offering the Methodist organ, on which Johannes started to practise one or two evenings a week. This was the same Dorothy Walls mentioned elsewhere in this book: she was organist at Water Street Methodist Church, Skipton.

At Christmas, Johannes asked if he might play the organ during a service. A teenage member of the congregation, Billy Mitchell, watched the German prisoner walking to the organ, and remembers him "flexing fingers which had spent the previous week lifting roots from the fields. He played a line from a carol, then improvised for fifteen minutes. He accompanied the hymns splendidly, and after the Benediction [at the end of the service] gave a magnificent rendering of Bach's *Toccata and Fugue*, to an audience who remained seated, having been stunned into silence. The little man in the shabby battle-dress left the organ stool and returned to the vestry, passing a diminutive old lady who said, 'By gum, lad, thou's played afore!' He had", adds Mr Mitchell, "in a cathedral in Germany." [Quoted with the author's permission from *A Dalesman's Diary, 1988,* by Dr W.R. Mitchell, MBE.]

POW Johannes Baumann in the garden of the Walls' family home in Skipton

This was not the first time Johannes' wonderful playing had been heard in the churches of West Yorkshire. When he played at Skipton Parish Church for a Good Friday service in 1946 he had to be escorted by the camp padre, as a prisoner was not really allowed such freedom. Later he gave a recital there as well as at the Methodist

Church, after which it was reported that he "delighted the large congregation with the quality of his execution and demonstrated his own versatility by playing several of his own compositions". His fame spread to Keighley, 10 miles away in one direction and to Settle, 16 miles on the other side of Skipton. The local newspaper reported that "an excellent organ recital was given at St Peter's Church, Keighley, on Sunday afternoon by a clever 22-year-old German organist and composer, Johannes Baumann. The recital was a fine illustration of the large organ, and his playing will be a pleasant memory to all who heard him."

Johannes worked with other musicians and with a choir from the camp, writing music and arrangements for them. The next newspaper report said that "German prisoners of war from Overdale Camp gave a sacred concert at Skipton Parish Church yesterday afternoon. There was a very large congregation. The programme, which opened with *The Trumpet Voluntary*, consisted largely of compositions by Bach and Handel. The concluding organ solo and choral items were composed by the organist. The singing of the German choir created a deep impression. In addition there were violin and cello solos, with organ accompaniment, and a Handelian suite played by stringed instruments." People did not pay to attend these wonderful concerts, but, on this occasion, a collection was made to be divided between the Save Europe Now Fund and the Parish Church Day School Appeal.

When the same group of musicians visited St John's Methodist Church in Settle every seat in the church was filled. Johannes was said to have shown himself to be "an accomplished musician" and listeners to have had the great "opportunity of assessing choral work, exemplified by perfect balance, precision and tonal qualities". The

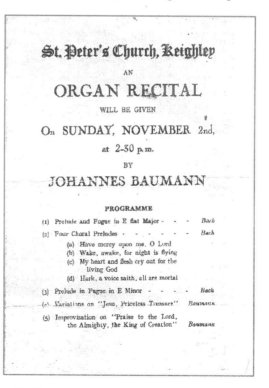

1947 programme showing Herr Baumann's own variations and improvisation

*Margaret Smith and her grandmother Bertha Hinde, with Maria and
Johannes Baumann in 1960 on one of their visits to Skipton*

settings were the organist's own compositions as was his final organ solo,
"Wie schön leuchtet der Morgenstern" ("How beautiful shines the morning
star!"). The camp padre, Pastor Wollenweber, thanked the church officials for
an invitation that had enabled the prisoners to worship with an English
congregation. A collection was taken on this occasion for the POW Welfare
Fund.

Apparently not everything always went smoothly with rehearsals and
arrangements for these concerts, and we can only guess at what was meant
by the words at the end of a newspaper report of a Christmas concert.
We are told that Johannes again "gave several impressive organ solos prov-
ing his complete command of the instrument. These included an original
improvisation on "Silent Night", a Bach choral prelude and the fugue
Von Himmel hoch. Expressing thanks at the close, the Rev. J.M. Roe ob-
served that the quality of the performance was all the more praiseworthy
because its preparation had involved difficulties and disappointments."

With their shared love of music, Johannes Baumann and Dorothy
Walls became good friends, a friendship in which Dorothy's family were
involved, including her mother, Bertha Hinde, and her daughter Margaret,
then a schoolgirl. When it was time for Johannes to return to Germany
they felt they were losing a family member. For his part, Johannes had
found being in Skipton an unforgettable experience, indeed he described
it as "overwhelming". Until he arrived there at the age of 20, he had in
some ways been cut off from the real world. Like many other German
young men at that time, he had, in his own words, "met mainly the Nazi
ideology, the main purpose of which was to separate the Germans from
the rest of the world. Their idea of relationships between nations was
based on aggression and terror." He felt that in Skipton he had entered
a quite different world. There people behaved in a very friendly way to
him without any sign of mistrust.

As soon as possible after his repatriation to Germany, Johannes returned to Skipton with his new wife, Maria, the first of many visits over the years. He now explains that because the friendship with the Walls family was such a great treasure to him, he had to tell his wife and eventually his children all about it. Dorothy Walls went to stay with them in Germany, becoming very fond of Johannes' mother and sister.

In 1961, when Johannes heard that Dorothy's daughter Margaret was to be married to Trevor Smith, he telephoned to ask who was playing for the wedding. "Your mother won't want to play," he said, "I'll come." Needless to say the music at the wedding was magnificent. Trevor was almost disappointed when his bride arrived at the church, as he was so much enjoying listening to the music they had asked Johannes to play!

Johannes fulfilled his determined desire to become a professional church musician. For many years he was the organist at St Michael's Church in Hildesheim, south of Hanover. He and Maria had five musical children, the eldest of whom, Ruth, visited Skipton several times during her school and university days. During such stays she discovered such a love of the English language that she became a teacher of English and music. Johannes is pleased to think of this as a consequence of his time in Skipton as a prisoner of war. Margaret and Trevor, and their children often went together to stay with their friends in Germany, and their daughter Alison went on her own to improve her spoken German.

On Johannes' return visits to Skipton, which he describes as "the very beautiful central town of the Yorkshire Dales", he has spent many happy hours renewing his acquaintance with Yorkshire's abbeys and priories. During his POW days he grew very fond of them, especially Bolton Abbey which lies only five miles east of Skipton.

Johannes Baumann, his sister Irene, Dorothy Walls, Maria Baumann and her children in about 1962 on one of Mrs Walls' visits to Hanover. Ruth Baumann is at the front left

Johannes Baumann, with his daughter Ruth Blüehm, granddaughter Corinna, Margaret Smith and Maria Baumann, during Margaret and Trevor Smith's visit to Bremen in April 2001

Another of Herr Baumann's interests is the relationship between Latvia, his birthplace, and Germany. He has translated all the texts of 500 Bach cantatas for use on Latvian radio, and even now, well into his 70s, he regularly translates Lutheran church information from German into the Latvian language. For this tireless work, he has been given the highest honour that Latvia awards.

During Margaret and Trevor Smith's visit to Bremen in April 2001, they met for the first time Ruth's 13-year-old daughter, Corinna. This means that the family connections have now spread to five generations, from Margaret's grandmother to Johannes' granddaughter. Margaret and Trevor enjoyed five days of wonderful hospitality, with much conversation about music, the church and their respective families. They report that

it was a much treasured time for all of us. We feel very proud and very privileged to have retained a wonderful friendship through five generations. A great deal of good came out of all the heartache and anxiety of the war.

Johannes Baumann has the last word:

I have learned that relationship and friendship between people and nations may develop only through a close connection and a permanent dialogue. For this school of life I am deeply thankful to my dear friends and to so many people in Skipton. Perhaps they may not be aware of the gifts they have given to me and to many other prisoners of war. These spontaneous gifts are the greatest treasures that anyone may receive during his life. It is over 50 years since I left England, but I shall never forget this time which has so influenced all the rest of my life.

12. Shattered Dreams

Chaddlewood House, an early nineteenth-century mansion in the centre of Plympton near Plymouth in Devon, had often been used as an army camp over the years. After the end of the Second World War, German prisoners arrived there, and quickly started a choir. They sang at Swarthmore Hall and Nazareth House Orphanage in Plymouth, as well as at the Methodist Church and the Church of Our Lady of Lourdes in Plympton.

Dorothy Coombes was present at the POW choir's first visit to Our Lady of Lourdes when they sang Christmas morning Mass in 1946. Their singing was breathtaking in its beauty. After this, the camp choir was asked to sing for Mass on alternate Sundays, interchanging with the church's own much smaller choir of which 23-year-old Dorothy was a member. The quality of their music added a new dimension to the services. Soon afterwards, some members of the church choir asked Father Moore the choirmaster if the two choirs could combine and sing Mass together every week. This daring suggestion was put to the rest of the church choir and one member summed up their feelings by saying, "If anyone objects because of the past events they have no right to be in God's house". There were still strong memories of "praying our way through air raids, feeling helpless and vulnerable as hell broke loose around us", but even so forgiveness was now the uppermost feeling.

This move to a joint choir proved to be an excellent way of building bridges between former enemies. Joint choir practices took place on Saturday afternoons until the men were allowed out of the camp in evenings, and by this time everyone had come to recognise the

Chaddlewood House, Plympton, used as a POW camp

Camp choir with children of Nazareth House Orphanage, Plymouth, 1947

superior musical skills of the prisoners. First, the church organist asked the camp organist, Franz, to take over the organ; then the church choirmaster, Father Moore, asked the camp choirmaster, Joseph, to take his own place. Joseph made the singers work very hard at their weekly practice, and the congregation were amazed at the resulting quality of the music. Services sung regularly were Sunday morning Mass, and in the evenings Rosary, Litany and Benediction one week and Benediction and Compline the next. When a priest who had almost taken up a career as an opera singer visited the church, he commented, "There is only one thing wrong, you should be singing in Westminster Cathedral!"

The role of cantor was expertly sung by Henri, a prisoner who had been a monk for a short time. His explanation for leaving the monastery caused great merriment among the young women of the choir. He and another young monk had seen some girls walking past the monastery, and they decided, so the story goes, that the girls had been put on earth for some reason, and they had better find out what it was. On being told this tale, Dorothy and her friends did not keep it confidential. Henri

was very red-faced when the next Sunday, Father Moore, in his usual humorous manner, remarked, "Well, Henri, have you found out what girls are for?"

Some members of the camp and church choirs on a Sunday evening in 1947. Dorothy Coombes and Karl Hunn, back row, second and third from left

It seems that many other conversations went on between members of the church choir and the prisoners. As they went walks together after choir practice and evening service, they would become engrossed in all kinds of discussions, some about the recent horrifying years. Among the men were some who had flown over Plymouth with the German air force. They were staggered to see the destruction wrought on the city when they were "supposed to be bombing the dockyard". Dorothy recalls, "We quickly learnt that these were ordinary family men who had been sucked into a conflict that they too had never wanted. We also discovered that their lives differed from ours in the sense that,

Dorothy Coombes at the camp gate

whilst we had a democracy, their lives had been very much regulated by fear and oppression of their Nazi masters." The youngest men were confused by the difference between what they had been taught in the Hitler Youth movement and what they were hearing in the camp. Dorothy remembers spending long hours trying to help some of them to come to terms with the necessary changes in outlook. One of the prisoners was a Lutheran pastor who had been banned from his ministry in Germany for several years. He was delighted to resume his church life in the camp and at the Methodist Church in Plympton.

Sometimes church members brought civilian clothes for the men to wear so that they could go to the local pub, if they were careful to keep their German voices low. One German, however, spoke with an English public school accent. He had been sent to boarding school at Kelly College, Tavistock, and was overjoyed when he found he was to be imprisoned less than 20 miles from his old school. On a return visit to Tavistock he received a warm welcome from the school and from friends he had made as a boy in the town.

The prisoners somehow managed to look relatively smart in their prison uniforms, and one day Dorothy discovered their secret. They placed their clothes carefully each night under their mattress. They were also good at making "something out of nothing" such as wooden toys and cord slippers which their English friends were delighted to buy.

In time, as the young women and the men built special relationships, Dorothy became close to two men who were both qualified medical doctors and surgeons. One was the outgoing and very handsome Georg Bohm from Munich, who, while fighting in the Channel Islands, had heard the enemy approaching and had given himself up by going out to meet them with characteristic bravado. He received numerous letters from places he had visited with the German army, no doubt having left many broken hearts along the way. By contrast, 30-year-old Karl Hunn from Freiburg, captured in Normandy, was quiet, reserved and studious, but he had great depth of feeling and was very loving. To Dorothy these qualities were appealing. She discovered that Karl's father had been killed

Georg Bohm in 1947

in the First World War; her own father had died as a result of gas poisoning sustained during that war. As Karl and Dorothy's friendship developed and deepened into what she calls a first class romance, they made plans for a future together. As she puts it now, "Karl had my heart in no small measure".

Because Karl was a doctor he was asked to see sick prisoners at Yelverton Camp, a few miles north of Plymouth, and also in two wards allocated for prisoners at the Royal Naval Hospital in Plymouth. Dorothy worked near Plymouth Hoe as a civil servant in the telephone manager's office, so sometimes the two would be able to meet at lunch time and eat pies together

Karl Hunn at Rusty Anchor on Plymouth Hoe one lunch time

on the grass or near "Rusty Anchor" on the Hoe. One day Karl pointed to something out at sea asking, "What's that? What is that?" It dawned upon Dorothy that, as he had never before lived by the coast, it was his first sight of a submarine.

By Christmas 1947 guards at Chaddlewood House Camp were on good terms with the prisoners, and a Christmas party was arranged to start on Christmas Eve at 12 noon. The choir was due to sing at midnight Mass, but by 11:30 pm many of them were still enjoying the party and had not arrived at the church, in particular Joseph and Franz, the choirmaster and organist. Just before midnight they charged into the building, and

Franz began to take out the organ keys, one by one, to clean them, seemingly unaware of Time, which was said to be of little consequence to him! Somehow the organ was in one piece when Mass began, and the music was as wonderful as ever. That occasion was very memorable, especially for the Christmas motets and the moving experience of everyone singing together "Stille Nacht" in German.

After the midnight service, Dorothy's mother and stepfather invited Karl and Franz back to their house for refreshments. It was not until 4:30 am that they returned to camp on that Christmas morning, singing "Hark the Herald Angels Sing" rather too loudly!

When the men were due to leave Plympton, those who had been regular attenders at Our Lady of Lourdes were presented with small gifts. Karl received a prayer book, pocket sized for ease of carrying in the hospital or surgery. As the prisoners started to move away during the following spring they left a great void. However, bridges had been built between former enemies, and in various ways those bridges endured. Countless letters were sent in both directions between the choir members and the former prisoners. Dorothy sent clothes for the sisters of Willi Kleipass with whom she had shared a hymn book on that first Christmas morning; she tucked packets of coffee and tea between the clothes. She corresponded with the surgeon Georg and his new wife, and of course, most frequently, with Karl. Two men of Dorothy's acquaintance had lost their families in the war and felt no urge to return to Germany. They opted to stay in England and work on farms until they were permitted to embark on new careers. They married local women and in time felt more at home in Britain than in the Germany they visited occasionally.

Karl Hunn returned to Germany to pursue his career as a surgeon. Dorothy missed him enormously. Due to shortage of money and the difficulties of post-war Germany it was six years before the two could meet again. In June 1954 Dorothy travelled to Germany accompanied by her mother, where the long-awaited reunion took place on Freiburg railway station. Six years then seemed like only 24 hours to Dorothy as Karl handed her a dozen deep red roses with the comment, in his quiet way, "These can say it better than I can."

His family gave Dorothy a great welcome and some of them travelled with Karl and Dorothy from Freiburg to Nenzingen near Lake Constance where Karl's brother, Erich, was parish priest, living with his widowed

Willi Kleipass in 1947

Dorothy Coombes and Karl Hunn on Nenzingen station in 1954

mother and his sister Irmgard. The family accepted Dorothy from the start. One evening she was asked to teach them the words of a song they had heard the English soldiers sing. Dorothy found herself instructing the German family how to sing "Hang out your washing on the Siegfried Line"!

Karl was working in a hospital at the time of Dorothy's visit, but he intended to set up his own medical practice and have a house built so that he would feel in a position to marry and settle down. He did open his own practice, and he and Dorothy continued with their plans, but sadly their story was not to have a happy ending. Very unexpectedly Dorothy received a letter from Karl's cousin saying Karl had died. He had driven himself to the hospital in great pain, no doubt realising what was wrong. He was operated on but died four days later of peritonitis. Dorothy could not believe it. She was devastated. Irmgard and Erich sent her Karl's prayer book along with a letter opener from his surgery desk. Later in life Dorothy married and had a daughter, but no one has been able to replace Karl in her life. His relatives still regard her as a member of their family and she treasures their love and friendship. One of Karl's nieces was named Dorothe.

Twenty years later, as Dorothy was in a waiting room at Plymouth hospital, she met a lady with a German accent, Inge Williams, who had married a British soldier. As they chatted together the lady was speechless when she heard Dorothy's story of Chaddlewood House Camp. She was the sister of Hans Horn who had been the camp interpreter and a great friend of Willi Kleipass. When Inge next returned to Germany she discovered that Willi, though married with a family of his own, had kept all the letters Dorothy had written to him after his repatriation.

A young German doctor, doing two years' practice in England recently, commented to Dorothy, "It is because of what people like you started that I am able to be here now". Despite the sad ending to this story, it seems that the building of bridges of understanding in Plympton at the end of the war was not entirely in vain.

13. Secret Bicycle Rides

Michael Betts never knew his father, who was killed in a road accident just before he was born. He lived with his mother and his maternal grandfather. During the Second World War, his grandfather, Mr B.C. Walls, was chairman of Skipton Urban District Council. He was an upright gentleman with influence who led the town in an enlightened fashion. Under his guidance, for example, the people of Skipton raised enough money to purchase a mobile canteen to be used by the YMCA in their work with British forces serving at anti-aircraft sites, in other home defence units or in their work with evacuees. The Princess Royal (Princess Mary, sister of King George VI) visited the town for the hand-over of the Canteen, herself serving the first cup of tea from it to Mr Walls.

Michael's grandfather was well known also for his musical abilities, holding the positions, at various times, of both president and conductor of Skipton Brass Band, and also choirmaster of Water Street Methodist Church. He was a gifted organist, cornet player and vocalist.

Being fully aware of Overdale Camp, the POW camp in his area, Mr Walls was interested to learn that some of the German prisoners there were musical. Once the allied invasions of Normandy had made good head-way in 1944, Mr Walls began to feel that it was only a matter of time before Germany surrendered. He started looking ahead to the time when Germany would need to rebuild its country and its culture, and he con-cluded that the musical talents of gifted citizens would be needed after

Left to right: Princess Mary, Lady-in-waiting, Mr B.C. Walls (Chairman of Skipton Urban District Council), his daughter Mrs Lucy Betts (acting as the Chairman's "Lady"), Rev George Speller (Minister of Water Street Methodist Church) and others

SERVING H. M. FORCES

*Princess Mary serving Mr B.C. Walls the first cup
of tea from the mobile canteen, bought with
money raised in Skipton*

the war. Most prisoners were sent out each day to work as labourers, helping on farms, digging ditches or repairing the roads, arduous work in all sorts of weather. He did not like to think that those with a special musical talent were involved in work for which they were totally unsuited, and which might well be harming their hands in the process.

Using his influential position in the town, Mr Walls approached the commandant of Overdale Camp to ask if it would be possible for a few of the more gifted musicians to have some time off from their labours to go to his house to practise on the grand piano and many other instruments in his possession. He was delighted when his suggestion was approved, and, of course, there was no shortage of applicants for these musical visits.

Michael Betts, a boy of 14 in the spring of 1945, remembers those days with these words. "I lived with my grandfather and appreciated good music, but I was a poor performer myself. I thus formed part of a small audience for many a fine impromptu concert, in which my grandfather, aunt and the rest of the family would join. Over the meals that inevitably followed we got to know some of these young men quite well. We found them very much like ourselves, full of fun and music and in no way militaristic or political."

The youngest prisoner, Geiert Meier, had been captured in 1944. He and his parachute unit had surrendered at the first opportunity, he said, on their first operation in Normandy. He was a keen linguist and spoke good English, but unfortunately he was judged by Mr Walls to be of only average musical ability. He was therefore extremely fearful that Mr Walls would not allow him to come again to his house and that he would have to return to full-time manual work which was not at all to his liking. However, a bargain was struck with him. Mr Walls would not stop Geiert from coming to the house regularly with his more musical

Michael Betts in his grandfather's garden

comrades if Geiert would be prepared to give German lessons to his grandson Michael during his holidays from boarding school in Sussex.

Thus began a friendship between Geiert Meier and Michael Betts, long before fraternisation was officially permitted. While the musicians practised enthusiastically around the grand piano in the drawing room, Geiert and Michael would sit in the kitchen discussing various topics in simple German while drinking tea or real coffee, a luxury to Geiert. In fine weather they would sit in the garden on deck chairs in the sun, enjoying Michael's mother's home-made ice cream, another great treat.

After these German conversations had been going on for some time, Michael's mother asked his grandfather if the two young men could be permitted to go out walking in the beautiful Yorkshire countryside. Mr Walls was not at all sure of the wisdom of this suggestion. After all, prisoners were not permitted to go about unguarded. If the two were seen it might put in jeopardy the whole programme of musical visits, which he himself very much enjoyed, and which, more importantly, he believed were extremely beneficial to the prisoners involved.

In the end, Mr Walls gave his consent on the understanding that the boys proceeded with very great caution. The house was on the outskirts of Skipton and so it was agreed that cycling would be the best option, enabling them to get into the countryside quickly without being seen by townspeople. Michael had a second-hand Raleigh bicycle. A woman's bicycle, painted grey in the wartime style, and used by Michael's mother for some of her Women's Voluntary Service duties, was unofficially borrowed for Geiert to use.

Their first expedition was, however, very nearly their last. After cycling a short distance

Geiert Meier on Michael Betts' bicycle

Geiert Meier and Michael Betts in 1945

they saw a large policeman peddling up the hill towards them. Although he was a little way off, his large helmet was unmistakable. In great haste, Michael and Geiert turned off the road, went down a lane and hid with their bicycles in a ditch, from where they were just able to see the policeman go puffing by.

Michael remembers his grandfather's reaction on hearing about this escapade. "To me it all seemed like good exciting fun," he recalls, "thwarting the powers-that-be if technically 'aiding and abetting the King's enemies'. But grandfather took a more serious view of the incident." It was decided that Geiert's clothing could easily give him away. He wore the prisoner of war's usual nondescript dark jacket and trousers with a patch cut out of the back of the jacket replaced by a piece of lighter material. For future cycle rides Geiert changed into some of Mr Walls' old clothes despite the fact that they were too large for him. Geiert was described as "a bean pole" compared to Mr Walls' portly figure. Another precaution agreed upon was that, if the two young men were stopped, Michael was to do all the talking. In spite of Geiert's excellent English he did have an unmistakable German accent.

Whenever the weather was good and Michael was home from boarding school, the exciting excursions into the countryside would take place. Geiert acquired an appreciation of the Yorkshire Dales with their many colourful moods, and Michael's schoolboy German improved considerably. As a bonus, they sometimes had a meal of fried bacon and eggs from one of the farmhouses still able to provide a high tea of home-produced food, with no ration points needed. Geiert had a taste of freedom, and Michael felt he had made a real friend.

One day in the Easter holidays shortly before the war ended, Michael was taken by his mother to a special exhibition of wartime photographs held at Brown and Muff's department store in Bradford. He had looked forward to a splendid day out, a long ride on a double-decker bus follow-ed by his favourite meal of fish and chips in Brown and Muff's "posh" restaurant on the top floor of the store. However, the exhibition turned out to be a great shock to all those who had queued patiently to see it. On both sides of a long corridor were displayed the latest photographs from Buchenwald and Bergen-Belsen concentration camps. As Dr Michael Betts now remembers it, "We were surrounded by death in all its most ghastly and hitherto unimaginable forms. There were bodies both dead and living so emaciated that they were all like skeletons. There were no captions – none was needed. Each photograph was quite specific enough in itself. It is impossible to remember all the photographs; one would choose not to remember any." The favourite meal was foregone, and there was not much conversation on the bus going home. Michael and his mother had been rendered nearly speechless by what they had seen.

Shortly afterwards, Michael returned to his boarding school in Sussex where he spent time in the library looking at the newspaper reports of concentration camps. He concluded that the Brown and Muff's exhibition had not been some kind of ploy to bring customers into the store but had illustrated the truth only too vividly. He became apprehensive about his return to Skipton at the end of term, and as to what his attitude should be to the musical prisoners and to Geiert in particular. Had Geiert really surrendered at the first opportunity or had he been involved in the atrocities of war? He had never been willing to talk much about those days. However, on returning home, Michael found that his grandfather's attitudes to the prisoners had not changed though perhaps the policy of non-fraternisation was more strictly enforced until its official relaxation in the following year. Mr Walls, a man of unbridled goodwill toward the human race, no doubt realised what Michael came to appreciate later in life, that it is not right to condemn individuals because of their membership of a particular race.

Just before he left Skipton to return to Germany, Geiert gave Michael a photograph of himself taken outside the camp. On the back he wrote, *"Für erinnerung an deinen Freund Geiert Meier, Skipton, den 30.4.47"* "As a reminder of your friend Geiert Meier, Skipton, 30.4.47." This simple photograph has indeed acted as a reminder for well over half a century, a testimony to an exciting and unexpected friendship between two boys whose nations were at war. Dr Betts, now living in Canada, has kept the photograph with other treasures from his youth. He looks back with delight on the memory of the close companionship he found while enjoying those secret bicycle rides of 1945. His thought now is, "Wherever you are, Geiert, in life or in death, I wish you well."

Signed photograph of Geiert Meier outside Overdale Camp, Skipton, 30 April 1947

14. A Helping Hand

In the eighteenth century Adam Bolz, a blacksmith, joined a mass emigration from Ulm in Germany due to famine. He and his family obtained 10 acres of land and settled at Novi Sove near Novi Sad, 50 miles northwest of Belgrade, in what became Yugoslavia. Two centuries later, in 1922, Stefan was born into the family, which was still German-speaking. In due course, he and his peers were expected to join the German army, so in 1942 Stefan Bolz and his school friend Philip Mensinger were sent to Munich for enrolment. The two young men hoped to stay together, but, after a doctor had examined them, Stefan was told to stand on the left and Philip on the right. The friends were separated. Years later Stefan heard that Philip had been sent as a guard to Auschwitz. For the part he played in the concentration camp he was subsequently given five years imprisonment, and two years after his release he died.

But what became of Stefan? He was sent to France for tank training and was kitted out with uniform suitable for service in Africa, but at the last minute his division was diverted to the Ukraine in this very unsuitable clothing. They were involved in the recapture of Kharkov from the Russians and a three-day tank battle at Belgorod over the Russian border. Stefan saw the terrible effects of war on both troops and civilians. Although the Germans won these battles they then retreated through the Ukraine and over the mountains into Romania. At this point Stefan had to abandon the small T4 tank he drove as it was no longer repairable.

Driving and maintaining vehicles became Stefan's speciality, as he had had some suitable training and experience before leaving home. Eventually he was appointed chauffeur to his Commanding Officer, and, as the Russians came nearer, he took his CO's advice, escaped in a Volkswagen and gave himself up to the Americans in early 1945. Along with many other prisoners Stefan was then sent by lorry to Belgium and from there shipped to Hull.

Arriving in England
His first British camp was in Crumpsall near Manchester. The war came to an end, and Britain needed to increase her stock of houses. Thousands of prefabricated houses were to be put up in Heaton Park, and the prisoners, it seemed, were to do most of the hard work. The first task was to

level the ground for which an earth-moving machine known as a "caterpillar" was brought to the site. The Irish foreman asked who had mechanical knowledge, so, not willing to let a chance slip by, Stefan spoke up. He was given the job of "grease-monkey", greasing, cleaning and servicing the machine. One morning the Irish driver of the caterpillar did not turn up. "Can you drive it?" the foreman asked of Stefan. "Give me an hour", he replied. From then on Stefan became the driver for an extra payment of five Woodbines a day. When the original driver returned, *he* became the grease-monkey!

Stefan was by now picking up the English language. He recalls meeting the senior foreman sometime later and being asked if he was still driving. "Yes, I've been to Bury two times today," he replied. "Not 'two times'", corrected the foreman, "twice".

On being moved to Glen Mill camp in Oldham in March 1947, Stefan was again given a driving job, this time for the officers' mess. This was a good position: he was trusted and could go in and out of the camp without challenge. He frequently drove a Humber Super Snipe Estate to Ladysmith Barracks to pick up food. He often chauffeured officers to the Midland Hotel in Manchester for meetings, where he would be sent to the kitchen for a good meal. On one of these occasions he met an electrician, Mr Marshall, from an electrical shop round the corner from the hotel. Mr Marshall had stalls on markets at Oldham, Rochdale and Bury. Stefan got talking to him and showed him some slippers made by prisoners, which he happened to have in the back of the car. Mr Marshall offered him half-a-crown a pair for any more he could supply, for resale at the markets.

Never one to miss an opportunity, Stefan set about getting these simple slippers made in large quantities. He paid his fellow prisoners a shilling a pair (or cigarettes or butter), providing all the materials himself. Prisoners who had come to Glen Mill from camps in Canada brought with them Canadian army blankets which were much superior to the British issue. But in Oldham these thick blankets had to be surrendered to the stores, so that all prisoners had the same kind. Thus there were numerous such blankets in the stores which were not needed. The Irish storekeeper was a heavy smoker. For a packet of Woodbines he would give Stefan ten of these special Canadian blankets. Thread and needles also were obtained in a similar way. The blankets made good slippers with double thickness used for the soles.

One day Stefan received a message that Mr Marshall wanted a large consignment of slippers by a certain evening, and he would come to the road outside the camp to pick them up. The team of slipper-makers, chiefly a group of men who had been prisoners in USA prior to arriving in England, worked hard to reach the target. Stefan was duly outside the camp at the appointed time with the bundles of slippers, but Mr Marshall was not there. A policeman appeared on the opposite side of the road. As Stefan paced up and down, the policeman seemed to do the same. What was happening? Eventually Mr Marshall's car arrived. Stefan ran forward, and as he was putting the slippers into the back of the car he dropped them, spilling them onto the road. The policeman proved not to be on the lookout for trouble, after all. He gave a helping hand as they gathered up the bundles and loaded them into the boot.

A Friendship Begins
It seems that Stefan was rarely intimidated by his status as a prisoner, perhaps because his skills were always in demand, or perhaps because of the kind of person he was – resourceful, ambitious and outgoing. It was his friendly nature which led to his meeting with the Hine family, who were to play a large part in his life, and he in theirs. One day in May 1947 he kindly stopped to help Noah Hine whose van had broken down by the side of the road, a story told elsewhere in this book. The surprising help Stefan gave him led Noah Hine to invite him to his house. Mr Hine's teenage daughter Dorothy was in the back yard when a figure leaned over the back gate and asked, "Is this Mr Hine's house?" The man then tripped lightly down the steps leading to the back door, and Stefan was introduced to the rest of the family, Mrs Agnes Hine and their two children, Dorothy and Jeffrey. During Stefan's many visits to his new friends he and Dorothy became fond of each other, though she was only 16 and he was 25.

The relationship between Dorothy and Stefan developed, but unfortunately, towards the end of 1947, he was moved to a camp in Ashton-in-Makerfield and then to Huyton, 30 miles away from his Oldham friends. In Huyton several lorries drove prisoners to work on farms each day and home again at night. The prisoner in the office in charge of the distribution of the labour force was Werner Brix, who spoke good English and later became an export manager for Mercedes Benz. A fellow prisoner working on the farms with Stefan was Bert Trautmann, who was to become a well-known professional footballer, goalkeeper for Manchester City.

Stefan himself was a good football player, an outside left. At 16 years of age in 1938 he had been taken to Belgrade by a friend who was to play in the Yugoslavian team, Britain versus Yugoslavia. The day before the main match a practice match was held in which Stefan was allowed to take part, scoring the winning goal, bringing the score from 1-1 to 1-2. He was known as "Messerschmidt", the fast one. He could run 100 metres in 10.7 seconds. Now, at Huyton, he and Bert Trautmann were in the camp football team together and were both spotted by Manchester City and given trial runs. Bert was chosen, Stefan was dropped – because, according to Stefan, they already had a good outside left! Despite Stefan's many activities he did not forget Dorothy Hine; in fact he wrote to her every single day.

The next move was to a camp in Winchester which was sited near a deserted USA army base. Here prisoners turned their hand to making whatever they could. Some made cigarette lighters. Horst, a German of Dutch

Camp football team, Liverpool 1947.
Stefan Bolz sixth from right

descent and the best engineer Stefan had ever met, made a very useful razor blade sharpener. Together they built a sports car out of a scrapped armoured car found in the army base. But when it was complete, the British officers took it for themselves!

Stefan's turn for release came in 1948, but he had no home to go to. His parents were no longer in their own house in Yugoslavia. They had been imprisoned in a camp in Novi Sad under Tito's communist regime. If Stefan had returned he might have had to work for five years in a salt mine. Fortunately, the War Office gave him a helping hand. He was offered a job as a driver of a three-ton lorry for a squad of men disposing of unexploded bombs. He did this work in Portsmouth, Chatham, Northumberland and Guernsey, registering with the police in each area as a "Displaced Person". Wherever Stefan found himself he was not slow to put into operation some creative and money-making scheme which usually benefited all concerned.

Setting Up in Business
In 1951 he returned to Oldham and was lucky enough to be able to take lodgings in the house right next door to Noah Hine and his family. At last he and Dorothy could see each other again. By this time she was 20 years of age, and he was 29. But how could he make a living in the country he had decided to call home?

His first job was collecting milk churns from farms in Oldham, Rochdale and Littleborough. They were very heavy, and it was a while before he was able to swing them up to his shoulder, the best way to get them onto the lorry. Early one morning a dog ran across the road in front of the lorry. Stefan braked hard. Many of the churns fell off and flooded the road with milk. Stefan expected to be sacked, but his boss, Mr Matthews, only said, "It can happen to anyone. Carry on."

Stefan Bolz and Dorothy Hine in 1948

Stefan received a helping hand from many local people, the most significant time being when he was trying to set up a business of his own. It happened like this. First he got a job in a garage. Then he started going to night school in Oldham to do City and Guilds qualifications in subjects such as panel beating and welding. He did well in exams and used to help Polish students who had not understood all that the teacher, Mr Phelan, had said. Seeing this student's potential and knowing that he wanted to set up his own business, Mr Phelan introduced Stefan to the owner of a small car-repair business who was planning to emigrate to Australia. The business was in a double Nissen hut in Harpurhey, only a few miles from Oldham. The selling price was £350, but that was far beyond Stefan's means. Mr Phelan offered to lend Stefan £250, an almost unbelievable offer. Noah Hine lent him £50 and another member of the family, Auntie Polly, lent him a further £50.

So, through the sudden and unexpected financial support of these friends, Stefan was able to buy the small business, though things were very difficult at first. One of his early customers was a man with a Morris Minor which needed a new fan belt. This would have meant going to the Morris agents and buying a fan belt for four shillings and six pence, which on that day Stefan did not have. He improvised with a clothes line impregnated with preservative and a scrap of copper wiring. He returned the car to the customer asking him to come back in four days' time to have it checked. By that time Stefan was able to replace the makeshift belt with a proper one. That improvisation paid off: much later he sold this same customer two cars and his son a lorry.

Despite the many money-making schemes Stefan had arranged in his POW days he had never put money into a bank. Most people paid the new business in cash. But when Mr Collins, the local chemist, had his car reconditioned he paid Stefan with a £120 cheque. The previous owner of the Nissen hut business had opened a bank account for Stefan before he left for Australia, but Stefan put the cheque in his pocket, not being sure how to pay a cheque into an account.

Shortly afterwards Mr Ashburn, the bank manager, called Stefan into the bank. Stefan recalls sitting there in his greasy overalls listening as Mr Ashburn gave him a little talk about the £37 overdraft which the account now had. At the end of the talk, Stefan's hand was shaking as he took out the £120 cheque and handed it to him. Twenty years later Mr Ashburn said to Stefan, "You made a fool of me the first time I met you!"

After 18 months of the new business, Stefan took his old night-school teacher, Mr Phelan, and his wife, who was an invalid, out for a drive over the moors. Now ready to repay the generous loan, Stefan had in his pocket the £250 and more for interest, and he handed it over with his thanks. Then to his great surprise, Mr Phelan gave the money back to him. As he remembers this incident almost 50 years later, Stefan says he "cried like a baby", and, even as he retold the story, there were tears in his eyes.

Aims Fulfilled

When Dorothy was 23 she and Stefan were married. The business was now, in 1954, able to support them. Indeed, as the years and decades passed, it flourished, and the enterprises of "S. Bolz Limited" included not only repairing, servicing and spraying cars but a petrol station, renting out lock-up garages, selling motorbikes, lorries and cars, and even reconditioning Porsches, Mercedes and BMWs. In 1969 Stefan received British citizenship: he was no longer a "displaced person".

On his many visits to Germany he would sometimes buy a damaged Porsche, bring it back to England, repair it and then convert it to a right-hand drive vehicle. Even the Porsche factory in Fellbach near Stuttgart complimented him on the excellence of his repair work. Broken-down Porsches would be brought to Stefan's garage from as far away as London. One of the family said of

Noah, Agnes, Dorothy and Jeffrey Hine in Oldham Park in 1950

*Stefan's parents came to live in the flat over
the business at Harpurhey in 1966*

him later, "He could sell you anything." He himself is quoted as saying, "Everything's for sale but the children." In his developing business he employed some of his new relations, his brother-in-law Jeffrey and Jeffrey's wife Margaret. In 1989 Jeffrey and Margaret Hine bought the business from Stefan. At the time of writing, Jeffrey and Margaret's son Richard is now carrying on the highly respected firm of S. Bolz Limited in Harpurhey.

As Stefan was the only surviving child of his parents he wanted to bring them to Britain in their old age. Earlier, they had paid for their own release from the camp in Yugoslavia. They had then walked and hitched lifts through Hungary to a transit camp in Austria and, in 1955, had moved to Germany. Life had been hard, with nowhere feeling like home. In 1966 Mr Stefan Bolz Senior and his wife Johanna, came to England for the first time and settled in an apartment which Stefan had built as part of a garage complex in Harpurhey. Mr and Mrs Bolz Senior lived happily near their son into old age, he to the age of 81 and she to 94.

Stefan and Dorothy have two daughters and two granddaughters. In his retirement Stefan imports German wine as a hobby. Due to his own outgoing nature and through "some absolutely fantastic friendships", as Stefan puts it, the former war prisoner has made good in his adopted land. Distressing memories of the war have never completely left him, but he has proved that giving and receiving a helping hand can produce success and happiness.

15. Minnie Mouse
and the Candleholders

What worse luck can there be than to be captured on the last day of a war? This happened to Rolf Göhler on 4th May 1945. Then started his prison term at Nadderwater Camp near Whitestone, west of Exeter in Devon, which was to last for nearly three years. He was a single man in his early twenties who had been a hairdresser in his home village of Dölzig, near Leipzig. In due course, by attending a church in Exeter, Rolf became friendly with many people, including George and Phyllis Ching and their daughter Christine then aged about ten, to whom he became like a big brother. During his enforced stay in England, Rolf often visited the Ching family and went with Mr Ching to see Exeter City play football.

At Christmas 1947, just prior to their repatriation, Rolf and his fellow prisoners took part in a concert. They had made candles, toys and other gifts in appreciation of the friendship and hospitality received from local people. Many of the gifts were hand carved out of wood, such as the four-inch articulated figure of Minnie Mouse which could walk down a slope, given to Christine. There were also wooden candleholders signed with the prisoner's name and the date. Christine still remembers how beautiful the candlelit church looked (see colour photographs).

When at last he was free to leave England, Rolf had another very unlucky experience. He arrived home just too late: his mother had died while he was travelling home. You would think Rolf Göhler would want to forget all about the war. Despite living in the east of Germany, which soon became cut off from the west, the young man managed to correspond with his new friends in England, especially every Christmas.

More than 40 years later, with the freedom brought about by the reunification of Germany in 1989, Herr Rolf Göhler at last managed to travel abroad. He paid several visits to England and one of his two granddaughters, Peggy, also visited his English friends. Each Christmas some people have reused the home-made candleholders kept safe since Christmas 1947. When Rolf visited Christine and her family in 1992 they made a similar candleholder from a twig, with bevelled ends and one flattened side. Rolf signed it and then took home one of the two original ones for use in subsequent years, a poignant exchange of gifts. Minnie Mouse is also still in Christine's possession.

Rolf's visit at Christmas 1997 was a remarkable celebration. It was just prior to the 50th anniversary of his repatriation, and he was invited to watch an Exeter City football match. At half-time a voice spoke over the loudspeaker announcing a very special guest from 50 years ago, and Rolf was invited to the centre of the pitch.

Later, Rolf met two English men who still remembered him, Ralph Rogers and Graham Moore. He visited Whitestone to see precisely where the POW camp had been. This led to a good chat with people in the neighbourhood regarding some of the pranks in which the prisoners had been involved all those years before. Rolf took photographs of the site, but there are no longer any signs of its former use. His memory of the camp was that there was nothing very special about it – except, of course, the people of the area who were so very kind to him. It is for this reason that Rolf continued to visit Exeter until his death, to see the city again but chiefly to renew treasured friendships made over 50 years before.

16. War is the Enemy

When Marian Claassen Franz was a girl of 12 in the summer of 1943, German and Austrian prisoners with American guards arrived at her parents' farm in Whitewater, 35 miles northeast of Wichita in Kansas, USA. The prisoners had come from the nearby town of Peabody to help with the harvest, working a nine-hour day for which farmers contributed 45 cents per hour for each prisoner. The main work involved cutting, threshing and arranging cane and wheat in shocks, and also hauling manure.

Surprisingly, Marian was not fearful of these enemy prisoners. What terrified her were the US guards, especially when one of them demonstrated enthusiastically how to attach a bayonet to the end of his gun barrel.

At noon on the first day, the harvesters washed themselves in the farmyard and waited to be given some refreshment, perhaps expecting to eat outdoors from tin cans. Imagine their surprise when Mrs Claassen stepped onto the porch and, in perfect German, invited them inside to her table as graciously as she would have done with any other guests! Overcome by this unexpected kindness several prisoners wept.

Ernest and Justine Claassen both had parents who had emigrated from Europe. They had grown up in German-speaking homes and were committed to bringing up their own children to be bilingual. They had three daughters, who at this time were aged 19, 12 and 3, and one son aged 17. At the Mennonite church they attended they still had a German sermon once a month, and a German hymn every Sunday. This was as a concession to older persons present who did not know English well and for others who had learned to love the German hymns. The congregation was gradually making the change from German to English.

Mr Claassen had six brothers and seven sisters who all lived on neighbouring farms with their families. Despite the obvious friendliness of Mr and Mrs Claassen and their extended family, at first the prisoners were wary, and the guards were tense, bringing their guns to the dining table. Over the days, as they began to realise that the hospitality of the home was extended equally to friend and foe, the tension was gradually eroded on both sides. The guards no longer brought their lethal weapons to the table, to Marian's great relief, but left them on the porch.

Farmers employing prisoners were advised, "Do not enter into general conversation with the prisoners, and do not discuss anything of a political

Marian Claassen Franz and her father Ernest Claassen in 1981 in front of the converted warehouse in Peabody, Kansas, used as a POW camp during the war

nature, especially anything concerning war". This injunction seems to have been ignored by the Mennonite farming families. Mr Claassen translated as the prisoners and guards exchanged stories of their families and showed each other photographs from home. Some of the prisoners had been captured in north Africa during the Africa Campaign led by the German Field Marshal Erwin Rommel. The prisoners were under the misapprehension that New York had been bombed by Germany, an example of German propaganda, no doubt. They even commented upon how quickly it had been rebuilt! In other circumstances these men would have been visiting unspeakable horrors on each other. Here they shared jokes together such as the one about Italians, which was lost on Marian at the time. It concerned Italian tanks which were said to have two forward gears and four in reverse!

Marian well remembers another amusing story, telling it in these words:
One afternoon, to escape the broiling Kansas sun, the single guard for that day had gone to nap under the shady trees along the creek, leaving the prisoners alone with the farmers. Suddenly excited chatter erupted amid a frantic flurry of activity. The prisoners had spied a fast-approaching army jeep with its load of military superiors coming to inspect the guard on duty. Several prisoners rushed to the creek to awaken the guard, who hastily rubbed the sleep from his eyes and regained his watchful post. There were stiff salutes, the clatter of weapons inspection, some intense conversation. Satisfied that the prisoners would not escape under such vigilant watch, the officers boarded their jeep and disappeared as quickly as they had arrived. The silent tension of the field broke into laughter as guards and prisoners alike enjoyed the success of that close call.

Marian describes these days when the prisoners were with them on the farm as very exciting. She still has the red and white check tablecloth which covered the extended table when prisoners and family sat round together. On it would stand steaming bowls of mashed potatoes, fried chicken, fresh tomatoes and beans from the garden, corn and home-made pie. The prisoners were unaccustomed to seeing corn served to people and commented teasingly that "corn is for the cow". Popcorn was also something they had never seen before: they laughed at the popping sound it made in the hot pan.

Some of the names of the men still remain in records kept by Marian's father. These include Hans Pfalzberger, Kurt Bauer, Johann Muss, Alfred Martin, Herbert Heidrich, Wilhelm Ernst, Albert Peter, Hans Brandt, Siegfried Eckhardt, Helmut Drumm, Fritz Ringeisen, Berthold Schwarz, Karl Burtscher, Will Vasekindski and Hans Kowalski.

The prisoner named Berthold Schwarz, who had been a German officer, apparently got on so well with his guards that he was able to tease them. At the camp in Peabody he made fun of the wall which surrounded the activity yard. With the permission of the guards he showed how his men could quickly scale the wall which was supposed to keep them inside. He placed a row of men at the bottom, others on their shoulders and so on until they reached the top.

One of the prisoners made an aeroplane out of wood for Marian's cousin, and another made a drawing of the farmhouse. Scraps of string were used by the prisoners to make other articles, and everything given to the Claassen family was treasured for many years. From these experiences Marian came to the conclusion that the German and Austrian prisoners and the American guards were not in truth enemies at all, even though the two sides were still killing each other in the war in Europe. The real enemy was not individual men and women but the institution of War itself. This conviction was to stay with her for the rest of her life and affect her choice of career.

More than 370,000 German prisoners of war were sent to the USA, starting in 1942, and held in about 500 camps, such as the one at Peabody. Their employment in industry and agriculture substantially alleviated the severe domestic labour shortage in many states. The Americans provided them with adequate food and accommodation in line with the 1929 Geneva Convention relating to the treatment of Prisoners of War, as well as recreation and educational programmes. The last of the men were returned to Europe, leaving by ship from New York, in July 1946. Most were kept as prisoners in Britain or France before their final release.

Many former prisoners corresponded with their American "employers". One such German man invited an elderly American lady, in whose home he had experienced kind treatment, to his daughter's wedding in Germany. He was so keen for her to be present that he offered to pay her air fare. Some men were so enamoured of the USA that they returned permanently after the war. Many others have visited the site of their confinement years later, one of whom expressed his feelings in these words, "If there's ever another war, get on the side that America isn't, then get captured by the Americans. You'll have it made!"

The Claassen family corresponded with some of the prisoners they had known after the men had returned home. They even paid several visits to Karl Burtscher in Austria and Berthold Schwarz in Germany.

Karl Burtscher of Nüziders, Austria

Karl Burtscher lived in the village of Nüziders in the west of Austria near the German border and Lake Constance. When he was in Kansas he was thought back home to be dead. During this time some men from his area were accused of being Nazi party officials, who had lived sumptuously while others were in desperate need. They conveniently put the blame on Karl Burtsher, thinking he was dead, to take the responsibility away from themselves. As soon as Karl arrived home unexpectedly from America, as a free man, he was immediately imprisoned and ill-treated by the French for six months. When his wife and daughters visited him in prison they often heard him say, "If only I was still in America."

In 1957 Ernest and Justine Claassen and Ernest's brother Albert went to Austria to visit Karl Burtscher. They met Karl and his wife Ida, and their three daughters, Martha aged 17, born before Karl joined the war, Marlies aged ten and Ida aged seven, both born after the war. Unknown to the Claassens, Karl's wife feared her hospitality would not be good enough for them. She had prepared every detail in advance of the visit, getting out the best linen, dishes, silver and wine, only to discover that

Outside the Burtschers' home in Austria in 1957. Back row: Mr Ernest Claassen, Herr Karl Burtscher, Frau Ida Burtscher, and Mr Albert Claassen. Front row: The Burtscher children, Ida, Marlies and Martha. Picture taken by Mrs Justine Claassen

the Claassens did not drink alcohol! On walking into the house, the Claassen family were surprised to see their photograph prominently displayed. Mrs Claassen made the comment "Today our picture stands in a place of honour," but the unexpected reply was quickly given "That picture is always there." During the visit

Frau Ida Burtscher and Mrs Marian Franz, taken in 1992 in the same doorway where Mr and Mrs Claassen visited in 1957. (Despite the change in house number this is the same house.)

they were treated splendidly, an indication of how much the wartime friendship must have meant to Karl.

Thirty-five years later, in 1992, Marian (now married to Delton Franz, the director of the Mennonite Central Committee office in Washington DC), was attending an international conference on war tax resistance and peace tax campaigns, held in Belgium. She made arrangements well ahead that while she was in Europe she would visit Karl Burtscher and his family in Austria. Very unfortunately Karl died twelve weeks before the date of the visit, but nevertheless she went ahead with her trip to Austria. Marian was met at the railway station by Karl's daughter, Ida Fritz, at whose house she stayed for a few days. On the first evening she was entertained at a family dinner.

There she met Karl's widow, Ida, all three of his daughters, Martha, Marlies and Ida, as well as a granddaughter and grandson (see colour photographs).

The next morning she was taken a walk to see nearby views of the Austrian Alps. Then they went to see the home in which Karl had lived until his untimely death, the very house which Marian's parents and uncle had visited in 1957. The daughters

Frau Ida Burtscher (centre) with her three daughters, Marlies, Martha and Ida. The picture in the top left of the album is the one of the Claassen family which was hanging on the wall in the Burtschers' home in 1957

had not forgotten the family story of how on that occasion their parents had prepared every detail in advance of Mr and Mrs Claassen's visit. Now, Marian was the one to experience the splendid hospitality her parents and uncle had received decades before. During her stay the family could not refrain from repeating how much her visit would have meant to Karl if he had lived to see her again. Marian also visited Marlies' home where, over a meal, she met her husband, Bruno Martin, their grown up children, Sabine, Rainer and Petro and one of Marlies' grandchildren. Marian appreciated the beautiful winter views from the windows and took photographs of the snowy Alps. Most of all she appreciated the friendship showed to her by Herr Burtscher's family as a result of the wartime experiences in Kansas.

Berthold Schwarz of Ludwigshafen, Germany

When Marian's parents and Uncle had visited Austria in 1957 they also went to see another prisoner with whom they had kept in touch, Berthold Schwarz of Ludwigshafen. Marian herself hoped to visit him some day too. When she was at a conference in Tübingen, Germany in 1986 she would have liked to visit the family, but they were away on holiday. However, in November 1988 when Marian was attending a conference in the Netherlands, she travelled to Ludwigshafen taking a German friend with her to facilitate conversation. They saw Berthold Schwarz and his wife Gerda. Berthold and Marian had much pleasure recalling the days under the hot Kansas sun during the war when Berthold was a prisoner under guard and Marian was a girl of 12. Marian was able to show Berthold a picture of the building where he had been imprisoned as it still stands in Peabody today, now used only for storage. Berthold told how difficult he had found it to come to terms with the destruction of German cities which confronted him on his return from America. Gerda recalled her own experiences of the war in Germany, going repeatedly to shelters and having to deal with the devastation which resulted from air raids.

During this visit Marian was shown a plate commemorating the Africa Campaign led by Field Marshal Rommel during which Berthold was captured. She learnt that many Germans thought highly of Rommel, believing him to have saved them by his heroic actions. In fact even some of his enemies thought well of him as he was known for giving his prisoners the same amount of food, water and medical treatment as he gave to his own men. He was never a member of the Nazi party, and despite lack of support from Hitler he achieved continued military tactical success. Later, being accused of participating in a plot to kill Hitler, he chose to take poison rather than forfeit his family's honour. Herr Schwarz, along with many other Germans, goes each year to lay a wreath at Rommel's grave.

Marian Franz (centre) with Frau Gerda and Herr Berthold Schwarz in 1988. The plate commemorates the African Campaign led by Field Marshal Rommel during which Berthold was captured

By this time Berthold had completed a career with the transnational chemical company, BASF, at its base in Ludwigshafen. Berthold and Gerda had two children and two grandchildren. Marian and Delton had three children and newborn twin grandchildren. Meanwhile, Marian as Executive Director of the US "National Campaign for a Peace Tax Fund" and as their chief lobbyist in Washington DC had worked towards establishing a peace tax fund in the hope that one day US citizens would be able to have the military portion of their taxes put instead to other government programmes. She is also vice-chair of Conscience and Peace Tax International, an organisation representing similar efforts in other countries. As that organisation's representative she attends UN meetings of non-governmental organisations. Throughout this work she has never forgotten the significance of the friendships made with the prisoners across national barriers.

Marian and Berthold met once more, when in 1992 he was able to go to hear her undertake a speaking engagement near Ludwigshafen.

What happened on the farm at Whitewater, Kansas during the Second World War illustrates a wonderful truth. Where kindness and generosity are shown with a gracious spirit to foe and friend alike, man-made barriers can be overcome naturally. Sitting down side by side, sharing meals together, conversing and exchanging stories, – such normal activities bring with them not divisions and enmity but trust and friendship. Nationality is no barrier. Individuals are not the enemy.

After a full life, Marian remains convinced of the lesson she learnt as a child. The real enemy is not people. The real enemy is War itself.

17. Two of a Kind

Ernest Clarke served with the British Second Army in France and Germany during the Second World War. His Regiment was disbanded following the end of the war, and, after a brief spell in Brussels, Ernest was posted to Hamburg. He was amazed to see how quickly Hamburg had started to rise from the rubble and ashes of war, with trains running from the suburbs to the city centre.

As a 22-year-old in a foreign city he was glad to discover Wesley House, a canteen for the use of British service personnel. It was housed in a partially bombed block of shops in a picturesque position by the bank of the Small Alster river in Hamburg. The canteen was closed on Sundays, but a group of British service men and women used to meet upstairs on a Sunday afternoon in a room converted into a chapel, and the army padre normally conducted a service. One day they heard that the Lutheran pastor in a nearby German church spoke very good English.

*British service personnel in 1946 in Hamburg at
the entrance to the Wesley House canteen*

Left: The first of nine stained glass windows given by Günther Anton to St Mary's Church, East Chinnock, Somerset, as a tribute to the help and comfort he had found there during his time as a prisoner of war (Story 2)
(photo: Brenda Bickerton)

Bottom left: Window depicting the Archangels Michael and Gabriel, fitted in 1969
(photo: Brenda Bickerton)

Bottom right: Günther Anton's final gift, the "Agnus Dei" screen of glass bricks
(photo: Brenda Bickerton)

Above: George Harder in 1998, with his brother Herbert, and the ship in a bottle given to George by a prisoner of war whom he met while working at a lumber camp in Alberta, Canada in 1942 (Story 3)

Left: Tool box made by Oldham prisoner of war Franz Weitmann and given to Jeffrey Hine in 1947, still in use in Jeffrey's garage (Story 5)

Below: Mrs Renée Longson in 2000, still using the sewing box made by a prisoner during the war (Story 7)

Above: Arbury Hall, Nuneaton, in the grounds of which was a POW camp. Picture painted in 1947 by prisoner Pastor Max Killius, using pigments from plants found in the hedgerows. Given to Harold and Lilian Hall in gratitude for their kindness. (Story 10)

Above and left: Former prisoner of war, Frank Mansfield-Smith, in the garden of the Northampton bungalow he inherited from his English friend, Miss Caroline Smith (Story 9)

Left: Silver bracelet with filigree design, made out of a silver spoon by an unnamed prisoner and given to Ann Dowding, aged nine, in Hampshire (Story 21)

Above: Around the dinner table in Austria in November 1992. Marian Franz from USA, front left. Relations of former prisoner of war Karl Burtscher: Martha Le Douigou, Bruno Fritz, Michaela Fritz, Ida Burtscher, Marlies Martin and Ida Fritz (Story 16)

Right: Christine Harding with "Minnie Mouse" and a candleholder, both made by Rolf Göhler while a prisoner of war near Exeter. The candleholder is signed and dated Christmas 1947 (Story 15)

Right: Poster drawn by POW Harald Beiersdorf showing camps and dates where the Wellington Camp Theatre Group staged performances within a thirty-mile radius (Story 22)

Bottom right: Harald Beiersdorf still uses his POW bag to bring presents from Father Christmas to his grandchildren each year (Story 22)

Bottom left: The lid of a mahogany cigarette box made by POW Peter Roth for Margaret Stratton whom he was later to marry. It depicts the rising sun inside a heart, with a border of barbed wire (Story 24)

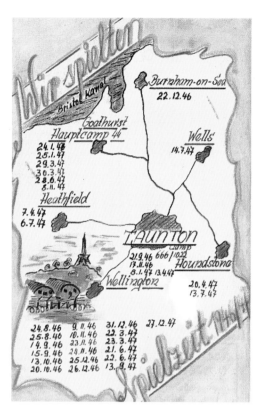

Left: The head of Christ carved in oak by a German officer imprisoned in Southern Colorado during the war. Given to Mary Degurse (Story 27)

Right: Photomontage by Kurt Geibel, giving an impression of Glen Mill Camp, Oldham, viewed from Greenacre Cemetery. It was one of the first Second World War camps to be opened, and ultimately housed 6,000 prisoners (Story 30)

Above: Reunion of British and German combatants of the 1945 Battle of the Teutoburg Forest, at the Reichswald Cemetery, 2 April 1997, accompanied by wives and friends (Story 20)

Right: Photograph stand made by a prisoner at Bedminster, bought at the door by Arthur Newman for his daughter Audrey who still uses it, and who is pictured here (Story 25)

Left: Welcome given by Fritz and Helga Kübler, in Oberheinriet near Heilbronn, to Greta and David Browning from Oxford in August 1999. David was taking the picture (Story 29)

Right: The cover of the Ripon Camp newspaper sent to Peter Heathfield of Essex by a prisoner he met in a café in Skipton, to help his understanding of the German language. "Die Pforte" (The Door) shows a picture of Ripon Camp and a door onto the world (Story 32)

Below: German classics printed for POWs, given to Peter Heathfield by Christoph Gaudlitz and other prisoners (Story 32)

Left: Sheet of all the postage stamps in use in Germany sent to teenager Brian Tighe of north Manchester by former prisoner Paul Ryschawy. The stamps are franked to mark the Prime Ministers' Conference in Munich, on 8 June 1947 (Story 35)

Right: Former prisoners who settled in Britain, visiting Brookwood War Cemetery, Surrey. Gotthard Liebich, standing second from right, with Heinz, Günter, Otto, Rüdi, Willi and an English friend Ken (Story 36)

Left: Gotthard Liebich dressed in his POW clothes for the 1998 exhibition in St Albans Museum. Wooden suitcase he made in Florida; US issue "Seasack" for transporting belongings, bearing his POW number; his English POW jacket and cap (Story 36)

Although it was against the rules to fraternise with the German population, they decided to invite him to their Sunday afternoon service. He agreed to come and asked if he might bring one or two of the young members of his congregation who were anxious to improve their English.

Ernest Clarke looks back to that first Sunday afternoon with their German neighbours in 1946 and remembers the surprising coincidence which came to light.

> After a most moving service, we took our German visitors down to the canteen (we had a key!) for char and a wad (a cup of tea and a piece of fruit cake). One of the young German lads made a bee-line for me. He had seen the insignia on my uniform and recognised the word "reconnaissance". We discovered that we were the same age, born in the same month, we had both held the same rank, and we had both served in armoured car regiments. We could name the same villages in Normandy. Had we met the previous year we would have been doing our best to kill each other. But that evening the love of Christ wiped away all animosity and hatred, and we became firm friends.

These almost incredible similarities of age and experience between the two young men, and their chance meeting led to a lasting friendship across the national divide. As soon as Ernest returned home to Thornton Heath in south London in 1947, the German Martin Scholtz made the journey to visit him and his parents. Ernest's father had served in both world wars, but when he met Martin face to face he could not help being friendly to the German.

Martin later became a banker in Germany and Ernest a Methodist minister in Britain. They both married and had sons, Ernest and Dora having three (David, Peter and Andrew) and Gisela and Martin two (Rudiger and Detlev). Over the years Martin often visited London on busi-

Photograph sent to Ernest and Dora Clarke in 1960 showing Martin and Gisela Scholtz with their first child, Rudiger

The families of Ernest and Dora Clarke and Martin and Gisela Scholtz in the garden of the Manse in Bletchley, Buckinghamshire in 1961. Photograph taken by Gisela

ness. Ernest would pick up the telephone and hear the familiar accent, "Hier is Martin." Ernest had no desire to attend reunions of ex-service personnel in Germany and even now finds it difficult to watch films about the war in north-west Europe. However, Martin and his family visited England several times while the boys were young and the older boys exchanged summer vacations during their teenage years.

This unlikely friendship, begun between serving soldiers of opposite sides, proved to be strong and enduring. Despite the sadness of Martin's early death at the age of 51 in 1975, the links between the two families still continue, a fine example of how loving one's enemy can become a reality.

18. Inside the Camp . . .
From a British Point of View

Peter Knight was just too young to fight in the Second World War, but his three brothers were all called up. The two oldest served in the Royal Navy. His third brother, Reg, was killed near Osnabrück in April 1945 shortly before his twentieth birthday, in what proved to be the last major battle of the war in Europe, described elsewhere in this book.

On leaving school in Lutterworth, Leicestershire in August 1942, Peter started an apprenticeship in engineering as a machine tool fitter at the Lutterworth branch of Alfred Herbert Machine Tool Makers of Coventry. However, when he turned 18 at the end of August 1946, he was conscripted for the "duration of the emergency", sent to an army training camp at Budbrook Barracks in Warwick, then to Stourport-on-Severn, before being drafted to Somerset to help with the running of a POW camp. On his way from the Midlands to Bridgwater in Somerset, a journey which was a new experience for him, he wondered how he would react to being in close contact with the enemy responsible for his brother's death.

The camp at which he arrived was in the village of Goathurst, south west of Bridgwater, a farming area. It housed about 2,000 German prisoners. The chief task of the British staff, which Peter was joining, was to keep the prisoners secure and actively engaged in productive work, mainly on local farms. Goathurst Camp also controlled satellite camps and hostels situated near towns throughout Somerset such as Taunton, Wellington and Yeovil, and in villages such as Crowcombe, Wiveliscombe and Cannington. There were many escort duties to be performed, moving groups of prisoners from one camp to another, or to transit camps prior to repatriation, and sometimes escorting individuals to hospital. The soldiers who acted as escorts were mainly from the Royal Pioneer and non-combatant Corps. At first the security was strict and escorts carried revolvers and live ammunition in the pouches of their belts, but soon after Peter's arrival the situation began to relax.

Peter's role as junior clerk in the orderly room involved preparing all the necessary paperwork for escorts, including travel warrants. Twice a day he had to accompany a German driver in a small lorry to collect the mail from Bridgwater post office and then ensure it was delivered to the right parts of the camp. The office mail had to be opened, booked in and given a reference number. Clerical work was new to Peter, but he

Aerial View of Goathurst Camp, 23 January 1947
(National Monuments Record. RAF photography)

acquired many skills which proved useful to him later in life. He soon discovered that if a group of prisoners were to be moved to Leicester on a Friday he could apply for a 24-hour pass and then volunteer for escort duty. This gave him a free travel warrant and the chance to visit his home in Lutterworth which was only 13 miles from Leicester.

There was one German clerk in the orderly room, Helmut Berger, with a desk of his own. He was a slim man in his mid-twenties, nearly six feet tall. His face was dominated by glasses with thick lenses, and he had a rather large mouth with big lips. He was quiet and did not mix easily but spoke and wrote very good English. Remembering these details, Peter now guesses that he had been a clerk in the German army. Helmut typed standing orders for notice boards, sometimes translating from English to German while typing. He typed with a speed which Peter says he has never seen since from a man! He was very polite and patient and was always willing to help with everyday German phrases and with other aspects of clerical work about which Peter was still learning.

As Peter was preparing to go on leave one day, Helmut trusted him enough to ask him a favour. Would he be willing to purchase a watch for him? With some nervousness he held out a handful of English notes, not being familiar with the currency. Peter was not sure what offence he might be committing, but he took £3, more than twice his own weekly pay. He bought a mediocre watch from a good jewellers shop on one of the streets in Leicester Market Place and gave it, with the change, to Helmut on his return to camp. Helmut seemed well satisfied. (Actually it was the same shop at which Peter was to buy his own engagement and wedding rings some years later!)

As an eager sportsman, Peter played in the camp cricket team, but during one game a ball hit his eye. The German doctor immediately sent him to hospital, and, with subsequent leave, Peter had nearly a month off work. This lost him his position in the orderly room, and instead he was asked to help out with a number of escort duties. However, travelling by train with prisoners gave him many opportunities for conversing with them.

On one such occasion he was escorting 20 prisoners by himself to a camp at Moreton-in-Marsh, Gloucestershire. By the time the men left the train, the winter evening was very cold with about four inches of snow on the ground. The four-mile route from the station to the camp went up a steep hill which was quite slippery, and some of the men were older than the average prisoner. Many had retained their own German kit bags which were large compared with the standard British issue, and other men had made suitcases from plywood sheeting. Seeing some of the men struggling with their heavy bags up a slippery surface, Peter stopped the group, and selected about seven of the younger men. He told them to go on ahead, leave their belongings at the top of the hill and come back down, while the remainder rested. When the younger men returned, he gave orders for them to lend a hand to their older comrades. In remembering this incident now Peter says, "I was not given to asserting my authority in any way, but, despite the sullen disapproving looks given by the younger prisoners, I was greeted with 'Danke, danke Korporal. Du bist guter Mann' from the older ones."

In September 1947 Peter was put in charge of the Motor Transport Office, a job in which his engineering training had at least some relevance. He attended to the paperwork relating to all the vehicles on the camp. There were between 30 and 40 three-ton army lorries used exclusively for conveying prisoners to and from the farms daily, and 13 other vehicles available to the British staff. These were five three-ton lorries (two Dodges, two Bedfords and a Chevrolet), four 15-cwt trucks (two Bedfords and two Chevrolets), two Public Utility vehicles (which would carry two people and some luggage or parcels), and two motor cycles. Peter remem-

Taking a break together, German dining room orderly with British Sergeant Major Patten and Welsh Chief Cook

bers that the 15-cwt trucks had two long portable seats along the sides in the back, and were known as "liberty trucks" in the evening when they were used to collect British camp personnel from outside the cinema in Bridgwater taking them back to camp after an evening out. Latecomers would often be seen running behind, trying to get a hand on the tailboard, knowing their mates would haul them aboard rather than allow them to suffer the four- or five-mile hike back to camp. "The most senior rank among us", he recalls, "sat at the front with the German driver, a privilege not to endure the exhaust fumes which always seemed to get sucked into the open-backed lorry."

Some of the vehicles were used for collecting rations from a food depot in the village of Langport, supplies required not only for Goathurst Camp but also for all its satellite camps and hostels. Other vehicles were used as personnel carriers or by individual members of staff.

To assist him in the considerable amount of office work relating to this large number of vehicles, Peter had the help of a prisoner named Fritz, a stocky, shaven-headed 40-year-old. Fritz's particular responsibility was the petrol and oil returns, and Peter says he was meticulous about his dockets. This was the first time Peter had seen a figure 7 written with a line through it. Fritz was an impressive person, always spotlessly clean and immaculately dressed with exceedingly good manners, courtesy and charm. Peter remembers how Fritz addressed him each morning, "with a lovely smile, a click of the heels of his highly polished boots, a stiff bow and friendly greeting, 'Guten Morgen Korporal. Wie geht es Ihnen?' (How are you?)". Always when Fritz left for his dinner break he would face Peter, click his heels and wish him a "good appetite" for his meal. Peter was still only 19 years of age and thrilled to be treated with such genuine respect by the older man. In return, he tried to put into practice the most polite German phrases he had learnt from Helmut Berger in the orderly room. Sometimes he would deliberately leave the office five minutes early so he could return Fritz's courtesy by wishing him a "good appetite".

Peter's work also included the daily and monthly inspection checks for the vehicles. This involved giving instructions to the German mechanics and drivers regarding the tasks to be carried out each day. This contact led to his being invited in the evenings to the drivers' rest and mess room to watch a German film. The room was big enough for about 15 men and provided regular entertainment for those on late duty or on a stand-by rota. Seeing the men in their own quarters led Peter to feel that they were ordinary fellows who had been conscripted into the forces just as British men were. They were eager to return home to Germany but were putting up with their spell as prisoners as cheerfully as they could. By this time, Peter realised that any apprehension he had felt when he arrived at the camp ten months before, concerning how he would feel about mixing with people in an army responsible for his brother's death, had long since disappeared.

The prisoner with whom Peter became most friendly was one of the drivers, Erich Rothe. He was not much older than Peter and was going out with an English girl named Margaret who was a friend of Peter's current girlfriend, Peggy Mayled from Bridgwater. Erich spoke very good English but with an American drawl, having been a prisoner in America during the war, and he acted as Peter's interpreter many times. On one or two rare occasions when Peter happened to be out with Erich in one of the 15-cwt trucks, Erich gave him driving lessons. Peter describes this now as "highly irregular, of course", continuing, "he let me have a go once just outside Taunton on the way to Cullompton. Erich said, 'OK Peter, pull up here,' and I did so without looking in my wing mirrors and with no signals. The bus-driver who was travelling close behind was not pleased. Erich wasn't put out and thought I did all right." Erich's home-town was Merseburg between Halle and Leipzig in the east of Germany, but he expressed his intention of settling in Britain when he was set free.

Peter had reason to be thankful to some of the prisoners over an unfortunate accident which occurred one evening when lorries filled with men were returning from their farm work. Peter was driving a motorcycle on a narrow, wet road going away from the camp. Knowing that lorries were likely to round a sharp corner towards him, and therefore keeping himself to the edge of the road, Peter skidded and hit a wall, trapping his hand between the motorcycle and the wall and damaging the motorcycle. Despite wearing thick leather gloves Peter almost lost the end of the third finger on his left hand. Fearing a possible Court of Inquiry, he ordered the prisoners who found him to tell no one. He had such a good understanding with the German drivers that they attended to the damaged vehicle by bringing replacement parts from the workshops at Cullompton in Devon on their regular trips. The German doctor who treated the badly damaged finger may not have believed Peter's story that he had trapped it in a safe door. However, as he now puts it, "All was put to rights, with no Court of Inquiry and a mended finger, thanks to the brilliance of the camp's German doctor".

Notwithstanding this and other mishaps, Peter rose from Private to Lance Corporal and then Corporal during his first year at Goathurst, and by early 1948 he was being trained to take over as Orderly Room Sergeant. In fact he did achieve the rank of Acting Sergeant, and it was during this time that four vehicles were to be delivered to Sudbury in Derbyshire requiring four German drivers and four British escorts. On mapping out their route, Peter arranged that they would pass immediately in front of his parents' home, a farm cottage just outside Lutterworth.

*Sergeant Peter E. Knight
outside the Sergeants'
Mess, Goathurst Camp,
Spring 1948*

This arrangement was for two reasons. The convoy would need to stop somewhere for a meal, but also he wanted to get his bicycle back home, having brought it down by train. Peter's pleas to the Adjutant to allow him to be one of the escorts were refused. Goathurst Camp was in the middle of the disbandment process due to the speeded-up repatriation of all the German prisoners, and Peter's work during this time was said to be too important for him to be away from the camp. Peter was keen to get a message through to his parents asking if his mother would mind putting on a meal for Peter's four colleagues and the four German drivers. By the time they reached her house they would have been driving for five hours. Peter's parents had no telephone, and urgent messages were normally sent in those days by telegram. However, the farmer for whom Mr Knight worked, Mr Clarkeson, invited the Knight family to send or receive messages via their telephone, Lutterworth 101. (No Lutterworth numbers were more than three digits in 1948.)

Peter did realise that it might be very difficult for his mother to meet and entertain German prisoners only three years after the death in action of her son Reg. However, Mrs Knight rose to the occasion. As food was still rationed, to provide an extra meal for eight people was a large undertaking, but neighbours helped out by donating ration coupons and food. When the day arrived all went according to plan. The drivers and escorts arrived as scheduled and parked on the road outside the cottage. The escorts introduced themselves to Mrs Knight who asked where the prisoners were. "Outside in the lorries", they replied. "Well, go and bring them in," said Mrs Knight, "there are refreshments here for them as well." Remembering this event, Peter now remarks, "This was typical of Mum, a very kind, forgiving and generous woman." After the delivery of the vehicles, the prisoners and escorts returned to camp, full of praise for the hospitality they had received.

Goathurst Camp was to close in the summer of 1948, too soon for Peter to qualify for permanent rank of Sergeant, but he was proud to go home with three stripes on one occasion, to attend his best friend's wedding as best man. After being demobbed the following January, Peter Knight completed his engineering apprenticeship with Alfred Herbert Machine Tool Makers, and he went on to have an important career mainly in the aircraft industry. He married, had four children, and played a prominent part in local government in Lutterworth and in Leicestershire as a whole. He held senior positions in the Labour and Trades Union movements, and was a local, district and county councillor. He was a magistrate for 23 years and twice held the position of Mayor of Lutterworth.

After his retirement, Councillor Peter Knight decided to revisit Bridgwater. He had written his "Memoir", a 15 page account of the time he spent at Goathurst Camp, and he wished to present the document to town officials and deposit it where it could be used for reference. He also wanted to say thank you to the people of Bridgwater for making him and his fellow soldiers so welcome when they were stationed there between 1946 and 1948. In addition, he took the opportunity to look up his old girl friend, Peggy Mayled, now Mrs Peggy Taylor, a widow.

It was November 1996, exactly half a century after Peter's first arrival in Somerset. With the help of the Western Daily Press, a meeting was arranged for him with the Mayor of Bridgwater, Councillor Ken Parkin and a Mr Willi Wontroba who had been one of the 2000 German prisoners in the camp in 1946. The mayor accepted Peter's historical account with gratitude, and it was placed in the Bridgwater Museum.

The former prisoner whom Peter met on this occasion, Willi Wontroba, was originally from Kissenbrück near Brunswick and the Harz Mountains. He had been injured and captured in France in August 1944 and at first was terrified at the thought of being a prisoner on enemy soil. After almost two years in various camps in England and a short spell at Goathurst Camp, he was billeted out to Temple Farm in nearby Chedzoy. There he built up a lovely relationship with the farmer, Mr House, and was treated as one of the family. They even gave him a birthday party on his 21st birthday, 1 October 1946 (which Willi remembers was the very day that Hermann Goering was sentenced to death at the Nuremberg trials). Not only did Willi fall in love with Somerset, but he met a girl at a local dance and eventually fell in love with her too. She was Jean Ilesley who, with her sister, had been evacuated from London to Somerset during the war. Because of the bombing, their parents also moved to Somerset and accepted Willi readily from the start with never a cross word being spoken between them. Willi and Jean were married in 1949, holding their wedding reception at the Smallpox Isolation Hospital near Cossington, of which Mr and Mrs Ilesley were caretakers while it was on standby, ready for use if needed. The newly married couple settled in Cossington where they still live. They have two sons and two granddaughters.

Although Peter Knight and Willi Wontroba did not remember each other from their time at Goathurst camp, as they chatted they discovered a coincidence. They had a friend in common. Erich Rothe, who had given Peter secret driving lessons and whom Peter had got to know best of all the prisoners, had also been a friend of Willi's. In fact Willi and Erich had been billeted together on West End Farm in Chedzoy in 1948. Peter had lost touch with Erich, but Willi still had photographs of him.

Where was Erich Rothe now? Neither man knew. Strangely enough, though, after the prisoners had been freed, Willi had bumped into Erich by complete chance in the town of Goslar when Willi was in Germany visiting his parents. While sitting in a café, Willi saw two men through the window, one of whom he recognised as Erich. The two men were fleeing from the east of Germany while there was still the chance to leave before it was partitioned. It seems that, after all, Erich's intention to stay in Britain had not been fulfilled, but

Willi Wontroba and Eric Rothe at West End Farm Chedzoy, in 1948

neither was he happy in his home-town once the two parts of Germany were divided. As the two refugees had nowhere to stay that night, Willi took them to his parents' house where they had a meal and a long chat before being given a bed for the night. That was the last Willi heard of Erich Rothe. Hearing Willi speak about Erich made Peter determined to try to find him again if he is still alive.

This 1996 meeting in Bridgwater between Peter and Willi brought back many happy memories for both of them. The headline in the newspaper reporting the event was, "Camp where Foes became Friends". Willi Wontroba explained, "The camp holds a special place for me as it was there that I first encountered Somerset and the wonderful people who encouraged me to stay." Peter Knight summed up his feelings with these words: "I soon realised that the prisoners were just men like me and there was no animosity, only respect."

Peter Knight, centre, handing over his Memoir to the Mayor of Bridgwater, Councillor Ken Parkin, with Willi Wontroba, November 1996 (Weston Daily Press)

19. The Prisoner
Who Lived With His Sister

A German soldier and son of a Lutheran pastor, 19-year-old Georg-Wilhelm Ungewitter, was taken prisoner and sent to a camp in Texas, USA. Late in 1946 he was brought to Britain, where, on arriving at a camp near Ruthin in North Wales, he wrote without delay to his family in Germany to tell them of his whereabouts. This letter was received with enormous relief by his family, especially by his younger sister Renate. She was about to leave home to come to England to marry a British army

Georg-Wilhelm Ungewitter as a prisoner of war in 1947

major, at the age of only 18. Major Tom Greenshields had been stationed in her home-town immediately after the end of the war and they had fallen in love. Renate was due to set sail for England on 18th December.

On the previous day, just before starting out on the journey to the coast, she received two pieces of news by the same post. First there was a letter from her fiancé giving the date of 6th January for their wedding. Second was the welcome news, contained in the letter from her brother, that he was now in Britain. Over 50 years later Renate recalls in her book, *Lucky Girl Goodbye*, how comforting a thought it was for her parents and herself to know that her brother was living in the same foreign country she was about to make her home, even if he was still a prisoner.

Georg-Wilhelm was put to work on a farm in Wales, work which appealed to him; farming was indeed to become his profession. He wrote to Renate expressing the hope that she would be able to visit him soon, as he was not permitted to travel further than three miles from the farm. Renate and Tom did make the journey to North Wales and went to the farm where he was working. There the farmer's wife had laid on a lovely meal for the three of them.

Tom Greenshields farmed on the family estate in Devon, where he and Renate settled down. In due course they were able to arrange for Georg-Wilhelm to move from Wales to work on a neighbouring farm in Devon and actually to live with them on their own farm. He was then in the strange position of living as a prisoner but in the home of his younger sister! He was released from his prisoner status in 1948 and returned to Germany in the following year.

Georg-Wilhelm kept in contact with the farmer and his family in North Wales and returned to see them more than once. However, in 1955 he moved to farm in USA, where he still lives and remains in touch with the younger generation of his former Welsh employers.

Renate and Tom Greenshields' long married life was spent on the farm estate in Devon where they brought up their five children. They proved to be an example of something much deeper than simple friendship which developed between people who were thought of as former enemies.

20. If Trees Could Speak

Part of the Teutoburg Forest

If the trees of the hilly Teutoburg Forest could speak they would have an amazing story to tell. This ancient forest, originally covering hundreds of square miles, lies in northwest Germany, between the Ems and Weser rivers, running south and east from Ibbenbüren and Osnabrück. The vast area of forested hills, from pines and fir trees at the top to oaks, birches, beeches and ash on the lower slopes, reaches up to 300 metres in height in places.

The story is told that in the year A.D. 9 the Roman Commander Publius Quintilius Varus, a relation of the Emperor Augustus, was ambushed with his three legions, deep in the Teutoburg Forest by several tribes led by Arminius, a German chief of the Cherusci tribe. The vast column of soldiers, women, children, servants and horses were attacked and killed among the swamps, gloom and treacherous paths of the forest. The Romans suffered an outright defeat which greatly disturbed the Emperor and put a stop to the expansion of the Roman Empire.

It is unlikely that this gruesome tale was known to the members of the 3rd Battalion of the Monmouthshire Regiment when they crossed the Rhine on 27 March 1945, perched on the tanks of the 15th/19th Hussars, and made their way northeastwards into Germany towards this same forest. Composed of both Welsh and English, the regiment spent the night of Easter Sunday in hastily dug foxholes on the south western edge of the forest not far from the small town of Riesenbeck. At dawn the four rifle companies were ordered to penetrate the forest, sweeping from west to east, to eliminate any German opposition, and leave the route to Ibbenbüren free for advancing armour and infantry. The distance they had to travel was two miles over steep and densely wooded hills with thick undergrowth. The battalion was normally carried by the tanks, but the irregularity of the steep ground of the forest precluded the use of any vehicles. They had to proceed on foot. Wireless communication was useless because of the density of the forest and hilly terrain, so the leading company was instructed to trail a telephone line.

The Easter Battle

The men started out in the grey morning light, advancing up a steep stretch of forest through bushy undergrowth and heather. Within minutes they were losing sight of one another, and a feeling of isolation enveloped them. Very soon their line of advance was barred by enemy infantry from the north, shouting and firing at the same time. Apart from an occasional German helmet appearing above the undergrowth there was no visible target at which to retaliate. In some places the bushes were so thick and the trees so dense that visibility was limited to only a few yards. Two of the British soldiers, John Gaunt and Harold Robbins, somehow managed to keep in contact with each other, and they, together with a few other comrades, reached their first objective, a high plateau. By this time many of the company were missing, wounded, lost or even killed. Suddenly, without any warning, there was another attack, this time by a strong enemy force firing from the hip and with fixed bayonets. Retreating quickly into the undergrowth, and not knowing how to return fire without hitting their own men, Gaunt and Robbins attempted to move east again, hoping that others who survived would do the same. Taking a narrow path they met two other comrades, Reeves and Mathews. All four unexpectedly burst free of the trees onto the edge of a deep valley at the bottom of which their tank support was clearly visible. A hail of enemy bullets killed Reeves and Mathews on either side of Gaunt, and he himself was wounded in the right arm. Tucking the wounded arm into his tunic and suffering excruciating pain while trying to roll back into the undergrowth, John Gaunt was again hit with a burst of fire through his right leg. He takes up the story.

Members of the 3rd battalion of the Monmouthshire Regiment, May 1945

Feeling faint through loss of blood and certain I was going to die, the sound of voices brought focus to my thoughts. A party of five or six Germans came to where we were lying and took any food or useable gear off the bodies of Reeves and Mathews. Robbins and the two Germans then helped me to painfully walk into their positions. Joining the rest of the German platoon filled me with apprehension. It was obvious they had no medical facilities, so in my weakened state I just assumed I would be shot. In fact I was treated very humanely with two Germans stemming the bleeding of my arm and leg, with some rough binding from a haversack. I was given water to drink to quench a raging thirst.

*John Gaunt aged 20,
March 1945*

Despite his state of pain and despair, John Gaunt was conscious of hearing continual heel clicking and disciplined communications between the German troops and their platoon commander, Lieutenant Friedrich Wandersleb. It seemed that the lieutenant intended to initiate a temporary truce, to allow stretcher bearers to pick up the wounded of both sides. John Gaunt thought such a truce most unlikely, but eventually British stretcher bearers arrived, guided into the German positions by a German who spoke some English. John Gaunt was carried out, with Harold Robbins walking beside him, down through a track in the forest, passing many German troops on the way. They arrived at their own lines, weak and shocked but grateful to have survived. John Gaunt regarded it then, and to this day, as miraculous.

But what is the account from the German point of view? Their infantry were all Reserve Officer Cadets, many under 18 years of age, but chosen for their qualities of leadership. Seven companies had marched for a week from their training camp in Bergen, north of Hanover, across the River Weser to the northwest tip of the forest, moving for eight or nine hours at a stretch, but only by night. Early one morning shortly after Easter, the leading group came under fire from British infantry. Wolf Berlin tells what he experienced as the members of his unit trotted one behind the other, not knowing where they were being led.

We attacked and suffered our first casualties. My brother Ernst, who was with me in the same unit, was shot twice through the thigh. Ahead of us the English withdrew, and behind us the trees were shredded by English mortar fire. As we were to hear later, our first-aid centre at the rear was also hit by several grenades. I stumbled through the forest with a few young soldiers, rifles at the ready, in the expectation of being showered by a hail of bullets from the bushes at any moment: a horrible feeling! Then we stopped. In front of the plain south of the Teutoburg Forest the clattering noise of the English tanks rang out. At the top of the hill several German soldiers lay dead.

Another former Officer Cadet remembers three companies marching the whole night through the forest. By morning they had reached a small valley between Riesenbeck and Birgte and were crossing to the next valley when British infantry posted in foxholes on one side of the valley opened fire. The Germans responded by posting a machine gun which provided cover for the Officer Cadets to attack with fixed bayonets and firing from the hips. The British retreated leaving their wounded and many supplies in the foxholes. There were bars of chocolate, half-used tins of corned beef and packets of biscuits. As the Germans had not had proper food for days, these items were seen as gifts from heaven. They could not resist helping themselves. This may have given the British time to regroup, but even so their wounded had had to be left behind. For the moment, the Germans were the victors, though they too had suffered heavy losses. They took the wounded British men as prisoners of war, not quite knowing what to do with them as their training had not yet covered that aspect of warfare, and they had no medical facilities whatsoever.

The Officer Cadet who was the "runner" for the only officer in the 3rd platoon of the 5th "Inspection" or Company, Lieutenant Wandersleb, was Grenadier Günther Scheffler. He had some knowledge of English learnt at

The remains of a "foxhole" dug by the Monmouthshires

school, and so he was instructed to set about interrogating the prisoners whom, he noticed, all had "Monmouthshire" shoulder titles. Many of them, and of his own platoon, were badly wounded. He continues the story.

The injured started to wail, as did our [wounded] comrades. We had no medical orderlies. We didn't even have bandages! Whose idea was it, actually, was it the Lieutenant's, was it mine? Anyway, as the "interpreter" I explained our situation to an uninjured POW and asked him, while wearing a white handkerchief, to go over to the English position, obtain a cease-fire and convey to his men our request that they should collect the wounded. It was because no German first-aid post was within reach that this suggestion was made, the unusual proposal that hostilities should be halted and all wounded on both sides be taken by British medical orderlies to the British first-aid post. Günther Scheffler left his cover with the young British prisoner, a white handkerchief fastened to his gun, and neared the British lines. The British prisoner took the message to his own Battalion Commander, Lieutenant Colonel W.P. Sweetman, and he agreed to it. The guns were silent, a British soldier with a red cross flag stepped out, followed by

Grenadier Günther Scheffler aged 17, November 1944

medical officers and stretcher bearers. Günther Scheffler positioned himself in no-man's-land with his white handkerchief, acting as intermediary and speaking briefly to some of the wounded, explaining what was happening. He showed the stretcher bearers the way to the wounded until the last of them, both British and German, had been collected and taken behind the British lines. Then he returned to his cover and shooting started again. By this time it was late afternoon and growing dark.

The surviving section of this platoon of Cadets had had to leave their covered positions on the slope because of attacks from British tanks and had moved near to the British lines where the tanks were unlikely to fire. However, their cover was too flat and stony, and they were stuck in small hollows with no possibility of moving and no chance of linking up with other platoons. In addition they were extremely tired after marching the whole night and fighting through the day. The temporary truce had been a welcome break for their taut nerves and muscles. By evening Lieutenant Wandersleb had been shot in the thigh, and all the platoon's ammunition had been expended. To save further useless slaughter they decided to surrender, and it was Günther Scheffler who was ordered to make this clear to the British. Because of the darkness, his handkerchief could not be seen, so he crawled along a ditch between the lines until the British could hear him shouting in English. Finally, at this part of the frontline, the platoon's struggle was over, and their captivity began.

The following day, after a night of torrential rain, other Officer Cadets took up the attack just at the moment that Lieutenant Colonel Sweetman had returned to Battalion Headquarters. The Monmouthshires' official account of the battle reads,

> Scarcely had [Sweetman] arrived when the calm of the morning was rudely shattered by a fierce enemy attack on the force at the bottom of the hill. The attack was pushed with great determination and left no doubt as to the quality of the German troops.

The Monmouthshires continued their fight until late in the evening of the second day when they were withdrawn and replaced by a battalion of the Dorset Regiment. Eventually a full brigade of infantry completed the task. By this time the Monmouthshires had lost 41 men, and 80 had been injured. They had taken well over one hundred German prisoners.

One British soldier recalls that he and his comrades had an admiration for the Germans they had been fighting because they had fought hard and had acted with such honour over the wounded. One German soldier remembers that when taken prisoner he and his comrades were given chocolate and cigarettes, perhaps in gratitude for their treatment of the British a few hours before. The Germans were grateful also that the British warned them to hide any valuable items such as watches or rings, otherwise they would probably be taken from them.

The Easter battles in the Teutoburg Forest were among the last major battles of the war in Europe. They were both the first and the last battles fought by the German Officer Cadets. They were the only operations in which the 3rd Battalion of the Monmouthshire Regiment did not succeed in completing their assigned task. The Regiment's casualties were the heaviest in any action they had fought, so great that the battalion was withdrawn from the brigade. This was the last battle the Regiment ever fought as, after the war, it was converted to a heavy Anti-Aircraft Regiment of the Royal Artillery. The Victoria Cross was awarded to 25-year-old Corporal Edward Chapman for outstanding gallantry and superb courage under fire in the forest, including single-handed attacks and rescues. It was in this battle that Reg Knight, mentioned elsewhere in this book, had the sad distinction of being the last man to be killed in action in the long history of the Monmouthshire Regiment.

This battle claims one other unique feature. As far as research has shown, it is the only engagement of the Second World War in which a truce was called mid-term to allow the dead and wounded of both sides to be removed. The Christmas truce of the First World War is, of course, more widely known.

Fifty Years Later

Almost 50 years after this battle, in February 1995, a letter was received unexpectedly at the headquarters of the Old Comrades Association of the 3rd Battalion of the Monmouthshire Regiment in South Wales. It was from Herr Günther Scheffler of Halle, Germany, one of the former Officer

Cadets fighting in the Teutoburg Forest at the age of 18. In his letter he outlined his part in the battle of 50 years before, as the one who had been instrumental in arranging the mid-battle truce and had, at the end, shouted out the surrender in English. He had been taken prisoner with no personal belongings of any kind, no watch, no baggage and no clothes other than his shell-splintered uniform, but fortunately he was uninjured. He then spent "one terrible year", as he puts it, in British camps in Belgium including the notorious tented camp at Overisje (known to the Germans as La Houlpe) where prisoners had to try to survive the winter with 12 degrees of frost and only two blankets. During this time he jotted down his experiences on toilet paper. His further two years in camps in England and Scotland were of rather more use to him. He intended to become an engineer, so working on building sites in Britain enabled him to acquire techniques and put into practice some of the skills he had learnt before he joined the German army. He returned home in June 1948 to Köthen, 20 miles north of Halle, in the Russian Zone of Germany where, after studying construction engineering, he made his career as a graduate engineer in Halle until retirement in 1991.

Over the years Herr Scheffler had often thought about the battle in the Teutoburg Forest. He had had no map or compass during the battle and was left with only a vague recollection of its location. In any case it was in the western part of Germany to which he was no longer permitted to travel. Not until the unification of Germany in 1989 was he able to start looking for the site of the battlefield. He had never forgotten the shoulder title, "Monmouthshire", and wondered if the former enemies might be able to help. Shortly after he retired, his old engineering office merged with a British firm and British engineers came to the office. A Welsh engineer obtained the address of the Old Comrades Association of the 3rd Battalion of the Monmouthshire Regiment. Although at first Herr Scheffler did not dare to write to his old enemies, he was encouraged to do so by a retired British officer whom he happened to meet while visiting the D Day landing places in Normandy. He then plucked up courage and wrote to "the brave old enemies of the 3rd Monmouthshire Regiment" to ask for information concerning the location of the battlefield.

This unexpected letter was passed to Colonel Myrddin Jones OBE TD DL, President of the Old Comrades Association. With the help of the Regimental Museum he managed to supply Herr Scheffler with maps and details of the battle which enabled him to visit the battlefield and find the graves of some of his comrades. Colonel Jones expressed his pleasure that they had been able,

in a small but not insignificant way, to further the cause of reconciliation, and also fill one of the many gaps in the history of events
which always occur during the heat and noise of battle. We feel we have
made a contribution, and are pleased to have been of assistance to our

new friend in his search for details of his first and last battle.

However, this was not the end of the matter. Herr Scheffler reports, "This was the beginning of a wonderful friendship not only with the Colonel, but also with about ten ex-servicemen." These ten members of the former Monmouthshire Regiment, who had survived both the battle and the intervening 50 year period, included two of the stretcher bearers to whom Günther Scheffler had spoken during the mid-battle truce, John McEvoy and Ben Rowley. Herr Scheffler points out that they were not medical orderlies but brave soldiers who had volunteered to cross the lines, trusting the word of the enemy. Although these two men have now both died, Herr Scheffler is still in touch with their families. He was put in contact also with Edward Chapman, who won the Victoria Cross for his part in the battle, Joe Logan, Roy Nash, Gwesyn Smith, Tom Lorryman and John Gaunt among others.

John Gaunt, in particular, was keen to respond. This may seem surprising as he now readily admits that with each battle of the European campaign, his hatred of the enemy had grown daily. He had felt that his chances of survival were rapidly diminishing, many friends being killed in each battle. The Germans were losing the war and yet seemed determined to continue the slaughter for no good reason. To John Gaunt, hatred, anger and frustration, to say nothing of fear, were ever present. In the forest battle this intensity of feeling, which his comrades shared, was unleashed on the enemy. He himself was badly wounded in that battle and only survived because of the humane treatment he received personally from the German Officer Cadets. His wartime experiences and injuries led to over three years of physical and mental trauma, during which he returned to "a semblance of normal mentality" only through the dedicated love and care of his parents. Half a century later he said, "The events in the life of an infantry soldier during the European campaign have not diminished in memory. They are indelibly stamped on my mind."

Yet, despite all this, John Gaunt was intent on responding to Günther Scheffler's approach to the Old Comrades Association, and for a very singular reason. It seems that Herr Scheffler was one of those who had taken him prisoner, and, as he arranged the truce during which John Gaunt was taken to the British first-aid post, he had undoubtedly helped to save his life. Now the two former enemies started to correspond with each other.

By this time Herr Scheffler had joined a group of 30 former Officer Cadets, survivors of the thousand-strong group of March and April 1945. Together they attended a Commemorative Service which was held on the 50th anniversary of the battle. Through some mistake, the Monmouthshire Old Comrades did not hear about this service in time to attend, and the British were not represented at it. This was perhaps an opportunity that was missed for both sides to meet. In his letters to Herr Scheffler, Mr Gaunt therefore suggested that the two of them should arrange a meeting in the Teutoburg Forest for all those men who had fought on both sides in the battle involved in the temporary truce. Herr Scheffler was not a stranger to acts and symbols of

John Gaunt and Günther Scheffler meet by the forest after 52 years

reconciliation after the war: his church at Halle was proud to possess a cross of nails given by Coventry Cathedral from that Cathedral's bombed remains, a visual representation of the desire for forgiveness on both sides. He was delighted, therefore, to take up this invitation to come together with the old enemy face to face, this time in a spirit of friendship.

The Reunion

The reunion was arranged for 2 April 1997, exactly 52 years after the original battle. Wives and family members agreed to accompany the men. As plans were being made, Mr Gaunt admitted to regarding the forthcoming trip with a mixture of anticipation and trepidation. Another of the Monmouthshire comrades, Welshman George Wedlake, said he knew it would be an emotional event which would revive strong memories, but after such a long time he felt it necessary to forgive and forget: he was looking forward to it.

When the time arrived, 15 former combatants from the British side, with their families and friends, a total of 32 people, made their way by coach to the outskirts of the forest near Riesenbeck, arriving on the morning of 2 April 1997. There to meet them were German combatants from the battle in question with their wives and families, Wolf Berlin, Wilhelm Finke and Günther Scheffler, and a select group of Riesenbeck citizens led by Franz Uphoff, who had cancelled a holiday to be present. There were many welcoming words, smiles and shaking of hands all round. The greeting has been described as that which one would expect from long absent friends. For the British, as ex-enemies, to be welcomed in this way was overwhelming.

*The piper playing "Flowers of the Forest"
at the Reichswald Cemetery*

The party first went together to a small German cemetery where an emotional service of remembrance was held for all who died in the battle on both sides. Wreathes and small crosses of remembrance were placed on the sites of graves. A Scottish piper played "Flowers of the Forest" on bagpipes. (The Monmouthshires had often been supported in battle by the 2nd Fife and Forfar Yeomanry.) There were tears in many eyes.

Next came a walk through the forest for the whole group. For the families and guests of the former soldiers it was a pleasant climb through a quiet forest, but they showed considerable interest in the past exploits described to them. For those who had been there in the heat of the battle 52 years before, there was said to be a feeling of eerie unreality. The British were surprised to see many of their own foxholes which had been preserved by citizens of Riesenbeck who pointed them out with pride. It seems the Germans had retained an admiration for the bravery of the British soldiers.

After several hours walking about in the peaceful forest and sharing poignant memories, everyone went to a hotel in Riesenbeck for a wonderful reception. Lavish hospitality was provided, paid for by the citizens of the town and neighbouring villages. The atmosphere throughout was one of goodwill and friendship. The hosts did everything possible to make their guests feel welcome.

The following day a more formal memorial ceremony was held at the Reichswald Cemetery where over 100 of the British troops killed in the Teutoburg Forest battle are buried. After lying in temporary graves at the end of the battle they had been moved to this cemetery in June 1947 (see colour photographs).

One person who could not be present was the officer who had arranged the mid-battle truce. Former Lieutenant Friedrich Wilhelm Wandersleb was by this time a retired Archdeacon but unable to attend because of ill health.

A British veteran places a poppy and a cross on a German grave

His remarkable action during the battle may well have been taken at personal risk of execution at the hands of fanatical Germans. It was at least partly due to his amazingly humanitarian attitude towards the wounded that now both nationalities had felt the desire to embark on this pilgrimage.

A 92-year-old German man, Dr Erich Roth, too infirm to attend the event, sent a letter and a book he had written. Ten pages of his book refer to the battle. He had been wounded and left to die in the forest till rescued by British stretcher bearers. Since that day he has felt thankful for every day of life left to him. Hence the title of his book, *Jeder Tag ein Dank* (Thanks for Every Day). His letter is translated as follows:

> I am giving you this book because on pages 5 to 15 it confirms the day when we stood opposite one another in battle in faithful fulfilment of our duty. In great respect for the British people and out of love for my own country I salute you from my heart on the occasion of your pilgrimage to the German battlefield of 1945. I owe the fact that I am still alive to those soldiers amongst you who did not shoot me. The same hands that carried deadly weapons now write to you in the comradeship of peace. Although I cannot speak English I still speak to you with an understanding heart. The language of the heart goes beyond the boundaries of sea and land.
>
> In the love of true humanity and with gratitude for the medical aid I received in the British field hospital at Rheine near Riesenbeck, Kind regards,
>
> Erich Roth (born 1905), retired priest and author.

Another German letter included these words,

> The purpose of our visit is to honour all those who died here so that we can shake hands with all those who feel the same as we do and develop a lasting friendship with them.

This moving and unusual reunion, of men who had been willing to fight each other to the death and yet were now shaking hands joyfully, naturally made headlines in local newspapers, such as "Return to a place of horrors" and "Bagpipes and tears of emotion in the silent forest".

Much has followed from this event, including a great deal of letter writing and the development of some deep friendships. Despite having been on opposite sides in a terrible war, these men had shared similar experiences. They knew what it meant to be cold and wet, hungry and in pain, under pressure to carry out orders whilst exhausted and in expectation of death at any moment. John Gaunt and Günther Scheffler have become the greatest of friends. Frank Wright and Wilhelm Finke have corresponded and exchanged photographs. A link has been formed between John Gaunt and Dr Wolf Berlin MD from Hanover who was captured in the Forest and spent six months at Edingen, a very large POW camp near Brussels, with little food. He remembers how the first ray of hope came to him when the YMCA supplied notepaper, pencils and books, which he describes as "a deed of unselfishness that I shall never forget". With this basic equipment he sketched pictures of his surroundings showing the small tents, no bigger than 4 metres by 5 metres, in which 20 prisoners had to sleep on tarred pasteboard. Dr Berlin, his wife Rosemarie and their daughter Ulla, have all visited John Gaunt's home

British and Germans becoming friends on 2 April 1997. Left to right: Geof Bunce wounded in the battle, Wolf Berlin who fought and whose brother was injured, Marianne Scheffler, wife of Grenadier Scheffler, and John Gaunt, wounded in the battle

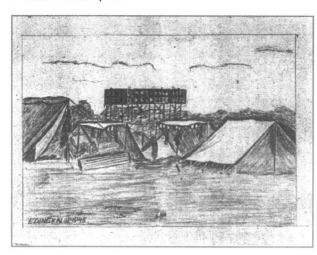

Camp in Edingen, Belgium, showing small tents in which 20 prisoners slept. Drawn by Wolf Berlin with pencil probably supplied by YMCA. Water reservoir for 12,000 men in background

in Oxfordshire.

Dr Erich Roth, the author of *Jeder Tag ein Dank* quoted earlier, wrote in one of his letters saying,

> Britain and Germany should never have been enemies at all. We have many common roots of culture, history and civilisation: this is to be seen in our languages. Monks of your country evangelised a part of our country. The princes of our dynasties often were relations. The last German Emperor Wilhelm II was a cousin to the British King Edward VII. Queen Victoria, grandmother of these two princes, set the tone of the second half of the nineteenth century in Europe. In spite of this [we have had] these foolish two world wars. But all of us who like peace and liberty are going to break with all these hostile senseless ideas with no future. We hope for a United Europe.

Participants on both sides of the battle have been amazed at the strength of the goodwill which has developed among those who originally met as detested enemies in the "place of horrors". From hatred and animosity has sprung a wonderful understanding and camaraderie. John Gaunt says that the reunion has produced "remarkable friendships and a deep understanding of life beyond politics, an understanding mostly missing from modern culture". His considered opinion, after much reflection on what has happened regarding the Teutoburg Forest battle and its aftermath, is that "If you can be friends after such experiences, you could in any circumstances be friends with anyone." If the trees of the Teutoburg Forest could speak, they would have to agree.

21. The Unexpected Gift

Mr and Mrs Dowding used to run Bockhampton Bakery and Stores on the edge of the village of Bransgore near Christchurch, Hampshire. During the summer of 1946 a group of German prisoners of war were brought to Bransgore on an open-backed lorry to clear ditches along Copse Lane, the main road into the village. A council foreman, Mr Young, who lived locally, was their supervisor.

Although Mrs Dowding's father had been killed in France in 1918, and her brother, an army officer, had been captured during the Second World War, she was sympathetic towards the prisoners. She felt they had probably not wanted to fight any more than British soldiers had.

One day she gave a packet of five cigarettes and a jar of jam to her daughter Ann, then aged nine, and asked her to take them to the prisoners working at the side of the road. Being known to Mr Young, Ann was allowed to hand over these gifts. Another day, as Ann and her friend Susan were cycling along the road, they stopped to talk to the prisoners. One asked their names. Because Ann's name was the shorter of the two, the prisoner measured her wrist with a shoelace. Ann was surprised at this and told her mother, who was horrified to hear what had happened, perhaps having visions of her daughter being dragged off. Of course, Ann had had no such fear, as Mr Young was always near at hand in any case.

Some time later, when the prisoners no longer worked in the village, Mr Young called at the Bakery and left a present for Ann.

The exquisite silver bracelet made by an unnamed prisoner

It was a silver bracelet with a filigree design and "Ann" engraved in the centre. The prisoner who made this exquisite article had been a silver-smith before the war and had made the bracelet out of a silver spoon. Ann was naturally delighted with this unexpected and attractive gift and wore it constantly (see colour photographs).

Ann and Susan have never forgotten the unusual happenings of that particular cycle ride, which marked it out as very different from their many other carefree rides in the Hampshire countryside. Over half a century later the silver bracelet, although too small to be worn, is still one of Mrs Ann Croker's proud possessions. Her only regret is that she was never able to say "thank you".

22. The Wellington Connection

Wellington is a small country town set between the River Tone and the Black Down Hills in Somerset, not far from the Devon border and easily accessible from the M5 motorway. An entry in the Doomsday Book records over 60 farmers in the area and 65 small-holdings. It is still an important farming area. It is perhaps best known for the person who called himself by its name and had an estate there, Arthur Wellesley who became the Duke of Wellington. His victory at the battle of Waterloo in 1815 is commemorated by the Wellington Monument, a three-sided column representing a sword, 175 feet high, which can be climbed by an internal staircase of 235 steps to a small viewing chamber at the top. It is positioned on the highest point of the Black Down Hills and illumin-ated at night as a landmark for miles around.

The town is also known for its connection with the Quaker family named Fox, to whom much of the growth and prosperity of Wellington in the last two centuries is owed. The Fox family developed woollen mills making the best West of England woollen cloth, so becoming a large employer in the region. As enlightened employers, the firm introduced old age pensions, insurance, free medical attendance and maternity benefits for their workers decades before the state did so. They also started Fox's Bank, built many fine houses and provided Wellington Park. Woollen and worsted cloth is still made in Wellington.

There is one story with a Wellington connection, however, which is not at all well known. It starts in 1929 when Brian Tucker was born. He was brought up by his mother, Gladys Tucker, and his maternal grandparents, Ernest and Alice Sparks. The Sparks and Tuckers lived at "Perry Elm", an attractive house and farm of 200 acres to the west of Wellington. In 1946 they were given the chance of employing German prisoners of war to help with the farm work. Brian's grandfather had been torpedoed twice in the First World War and had survived only by climbing a rope, something he had never been able to do before or since, but had managed when it was a case of life or death. Despite these wartime experiences Mr Sparks was not bitter towards Germany, and he decided to employ some of the prisoners.

Each farmer was allowed two or three men from the POW camp which was situated at Pyles Thorne on the site of a former army camp not far from the centre of Wellington. Early every morning Brian's grandfather would milk the cows, put the milk churns on his trailer, take it to Alpin and Barrett's Creamery in Wellington, and then pick up the prisoners from outside the camp in time for an 8:30 am start at the farm. The men would work

"Perry Elm" near Wellington, Brian Tucker's childhood home

until 5 pm each weekday and a half day on Saturdays. The cost for the three men for a month's work was £14 9s 2d.

At this time Brian Tucker was attending Palmers School in Taunton, travelling by bus each day. He sometimes saw the prisoners from the bus or when he was at home, although at first they were not supposed to be invited into the farmhouse, taking their meals in the dairy. As a boy of 16, Brian was a little fearful of some of the men due to their rough demeanour or seemingly arrogant manner, but others appeared more friendly or more educated. Those tended to be the ones who eventually were invited to lunch or tea at "Perry Elm" on Sunday afternoons. They would spend time in the garden with Brian in good weather and Brian's family liked to show them every kindness and provide a large lunch or tea.

The men, for their part, were more than pleased to make friends with the Sparks and Tuckers and other people who visited "Perry Elm". It did not escape their notice that Brian's family would introduce them as "our German friends" rather than as prisoners, despite the circles on their backs where different coloured material had been inserted to mark them out as prisoners, or the PW on the arms of those whose clothing had originated in American camps.

Several men became regular visitors to "Perry Elm". One was Norbert Baur from Stuttgart, a farmer's son who wanted to learn the English way of farming. At weekends he brought along his friend Harald Beiersdorf from East Prussia, and it was Harald who eventually became most attached to Wellington. Brian thought of them both as "real gentlemen".

Harald Beiersdorf had been taken prisoner in 1944 by the Americans in France at the age of 19. He had first spent over a year at a large camp in Sudbury, Derbyshire; it was there that he heard the news that the war in Europe was over. *Die Wochenpost* (The Weekly Post), the newspaper provided for prisoners by the British, carried the headline "Ende des Krieges. Die Kapitulationen in Reims und Berlin" (End of the war.

The newspaper which brought the news to the prisoners that the war had ended in Europe. Photographs show German Generals surrendering at Field Marshal Montgomery's headquarters in Germany and at General Eisenhower's headquarters in France

Surrender in Reims and Berlin), with proof in the form of photographs showing German Generals signing submission documents in both France and Germany. For several years this newspaper had brought wartime news to prisoners, written in an unbiased way, a free press, something new to Harald who had known only a press controlled by the German Government. Although Harald was glad the war was over, he did not know where his parents and sister were or where to call "home". He could only hope that the future would be good.

In October 1945 Harald was moved with about 20 other men to Goathurst Camp, Bridgwater in Somerset, and then shortly afterwards to the satellite hostel in Wellington. There they joined about 380 men who had been captured in Jersey and Guernsey. The camp housed 400 men in Nissen huts with 20 two-tier bunks per hut.

Altogether there were 18 huts on the site, one of which was occupied solely by men who formed a Theatre Group of which Harald was the Art Director. As an artistic young man, he applied his skills to building a stage in the mess hall, making stage backdrops and scenery for the plays, and painting posters to advertise the performances within the camp. The plays tended to be comedies or musicals about friendship or love, some in German dialect. They were taken from books which Harald obtained by post from the YMCA in London, or were written by the men themselves. One of the prisoners, Rudolf Eichelberger, wrote thrillers: he and Harald remained good friends after returning to Germany, Rudolf becoming godfather to Harald's son. The Theatre Group was allowed to stage shows for prisoners in other camps too, a time-consuming activity for the 18 men involved. During 1946 and 1947 the Theatre Group put on performances at Bridgwater's satellite camps in Wells, Hound-

Members of the Theatre Group with props, in the grounds of Pyles Thorne Camp. Gerhard Wördemann, Helmut Schäfer, Harald Beiersdorf and Paul Dorozalla

stone (Yeovil), Taunton, Heathfield and Burnham-on-Sea, all within about a 30-mile radius. They also paid seven visits to the main camp at Bridgwater and gave about 20 performances in Wellington camp itself. The British army permitted them the use of two lorries, one for the men and one for the transport of the stage scenery and props, the men even being allowed to drive themselves without a British escort (see colour photographs).

When the Sparks and Tuckers heard that the Theatre Group needed old clothes for theatre costumes, they and their English friends all helped, although clothes rationing was still in force. They found old furniture which could be used as theatre props, and, in return, the prisoners gave a performance in the camp one evening for these English people. They made toys and other items out of wood, even as large as a Bible box, deep enough for an old family Bible. Some of these items were given to their English friends in appreciation for their help and friendship, and others were sold for cash.

The Theatre Group very much wanted to take photographs of what they were doing, but no prisoner was allowed a camera. Then a sympathetic English friend loaned a camera to Harald for a weekend. Knowing they would be searched at the camp gates, they asked comrades who worked in the kitchen near to the edge of the camp to hold out an open sheet by the hedge which ran in front of the large barbed wire fence. The camera was thrown over the hedge and fence, where it was caught successfully in the sheet!

Harald still remembers one incident which made a big impression on him. One day in 1947 Brian was on the bus going to school when it passed a lorry carrying prisoners on their way to work in Taunton. Seeing

Harald Beiersdorf (right) with comrades including (standing) Heinz Behrend and Karl Weingärtner, in the grounds of Pyles Thorne Camp, Wellington. Taken on Whitsunday 1947 with the borrowed camera

Harald on the lorry, Brian waved, but Harald did not respond. When the two next met, Brian asked Harald why he had not waved. On being told that prisoners were not supposed to wave, Brian's quick response was that he would ask the commandant to permit it. Harald was impressed with the boy's immediate retort, irrespective of whether he took any action. To Harald it signified a freedom of thought he himself had not known. As Harald now puts it, Wellington was the place where he first saw, recognised and learnt about democracy: one can say and read what one likes in a democracy, whereas in a dictatorship one is allowed to hold only one opinion, doing what one is told without comment.

His two and a half years as a prisoner in Wellington provided Harald with other memorable experiences and some more new friends. The jobs he was given were farming and building. He helped to build houses near Sherford Army Camp in the south of Taunton, at which time he was introduced by another prisoner, Gerhard Oettle, to Mr and Mrs Marshall and their daughter Olive who lived in the village of Henlade near Taunton where Gerhard was working. The family remained good friends with Harald for many years and were to become the cause of his return to England at a later date.

Harald preferred jobs on farms as there was more food available in the farming community. He enjoyed the journey over the Black Down Hills towards Chard, in an army truck which dropped the workers off at farms along the way. He stayed to the farthest point, Halswell Farm near Combe St

Three prisoners with the Sparks and Tuckers at Perry Elm, Whitsunday 1947

Brian and Julia Tucker with Mr Spiller's son-in-law Mr Vile, and also Lilo Beiersdorf, taken by Harald Beiersdorf during his return visit to Hallswell Farm in 1999

Nicholas, where he worked for the farmer, Mr Spiller. There he learnt to milk cows, and he also plastered the cow shed walls with cement to bring it in line with health regulations. Mrs Spiller gave the prisoners bread and butter and sometimes cooked them bacon and eggs.

At another time Harald made hay not far from the camp at "Legglands", an estate owned by Mrs Dot Fox, a keen horsewoman, who needed all the hay she could harvest to feed the animals through the winter. She entered her horses in weekend races and Harald remembers seeing the trophies on Monday mornings, but, more importantly to the men, she introduced them to Cornish pasties! Another member of the family, Penelope Fox, remembers that a farm-hand thought that the prisoners would understand English if he shouted!

At Christmas 1947 Harald benefited from an invitation received at the camp for five men to have lunch and tea with two other members of the Fox family, Miss Marion Fox and her younger sister Margery who lived together at The Bower, Fore Street in Wellington. Marion, now in her 80s, had been one of a group of four members of the Society of Friends to be the first to enter Germany after the end of the First World War. Her nephew, Hubert Fox, later wrote of her, "It was her love for the old Germany and her compassion for the sufferings that war and defeat had brought upon that country that impelled her to devote the rest of her life to healing the wounds caused by this war and its far-reaching consequences." Between the wars she paid many visits to Germany helping to distribute food and clothing. Through relief and social work, her aim was not to show pity but sympathy and friendship. After the Second World War, Marion felt that all the slow work of reconciliation had to start all over again; although she was too old to return to Germany, she opened her home to the prisoners at the camp in Wellington. Even before fraternisation was allowed, when the prisoners marched to church, Marion made a point of standing in her window as they went by. In November 1947 she wrote to a friend, Mary Butler,

> My sister and I have the happiness since last Christmas Eve of
> sometimes helping German prisoners here 'to forget their captivity'.
> Many of them are such nice men. Most Sundays we invite two to
> tea and to sit in comfortable chairs by the fire. You see we can
> both speak German.

Harald was fortunate to be one of those who experienced this Quaker
hospitality. For most of this time Harald had no news of his parents and
sister in East Prussia (now part of Poland). Although he had sent a Red
Cross postcard to Dortmund in Rheinland at Christmas 1944, no reply
arrived until 29 March 1946. From an uncle he then learnt that his mother
and sister were living with an aunt in Brandenburg near Berlin. Later his
father obtained work with the police force, becoming a police inspector
in Hamburg, and the family moved there. It was to Hamburg, therefore,
that Harald went when he was freed, in one of the last groups to be
released from Wellington Camp, arriving in Hamburg on 9 April 1948.

On returning to Germany, Harald was penniless with no qualifications,
and his family were still refugees from East Prussia trying to make a
home for themselves in Hamburg. Even so, Harald started to save money
with the hope of revisiting Somerset one day. He kept in touch with his
English friends sending them home-painted Christmas cards each year
and, in 1955, a card announcing his engagement to Liselotte ("Lilo")
Schulz. In June 1957 he accepted an invitation to attend the wedding of
Olive Marshall and Bill Sainsbury in Taunton. After the wedding he
determined to seek out his Wellington friends at "Perry Elm". He caught
a bus the five miles from Taunton to Wellington and then walked two
miles to "Perry Elm", but to his dismay
his friends were no longer there. He
was directed to "Selby House" in the
village of Pleamore Cross, three
quarters of a mile away, and there he
found Brian Tucker and his mother,
who of course were surprised and
delighted to see him. They talked of
old times, caught up with each other's
news and went a car drive together to
the well-known landmark, the Wellington Monument!

For Harald this was the first of many
return visits to Somerset, and from this
date the Wellington/ Hamburg connection was firmly established. He and his
wife Lilo (and later their children,
Christiane and Axel) visited Brian and

*Julia Tucker and Lilo Beiersdorf
enjoying their shared
interest in music*

Brian and Julia Tucker in their garden in June 2000, with Lilo and Harald Beiersdorf and their daughter's family, Conrad, Cornelius, Catharina, Constantin and Christiane Fühner

his wife Julia, and their children, Julian and Angela. Letters were sent back and forth, not only between Brian and Harald but also between Julia and Lilo, who became good friends, having an interest in common, music. Lilo played the piano and Julia the guitar and recorder. As international telephone calls dropped in price, the telephone link between the families was used more often. Sometimes the German family stayed with Brian and Julia for a week: other times they rented a cottage a few miles away or explored other areas of the southwest. Over the years Brian and Julia have sprung some surprises on their German guests. On one occasion Olive and Bill Sainsbury arrived unannounced for dinner; at another time it was Mr and Mrs Spiller from the farm who appeared unexpectedly. At the end of every visit, Harald and Lilo said to Brian and Julia, "Please come to Hamburg".

At last, in May 1994 the first of Brian and Julia's visits to Hamburg took place. There they discovered that Harald still had sketches of stage scenery and posters he had drawn when he was a prisoner in Wellington, advertising the performances of the camp's Theatre Group. In Hamburg he had established, with a partner, a commercial art and design centre, with an international graphic design agency and school of 260 students. On their second visit to Germany only three years later, perhaps making up for lost time, Brian and Julia enjoyed a holiday with their German friends at a hotel on the shores of the Baltic Sea.

There is one way in which Harald knows he can never forget his years in Wellington. Each Christmas Eve he uses his POW bag when he dresses up as Father Christmas to deliver presents to his children, and now his grandchildren (see colour photographs). The bag is in good condition after nearly 60 years and is still marked clearly with his name and POW number, "H Beiersdorf. 812692". Then each New Year's Day he telephones Wellington to wish Brian and Julia a "Happy New Year" from their German friends in Hamburg, the first of many telephone calls for the year ahead, renewing the Wellington/Hamburg connection for yet another year.

23. The Lost Cigarette Lighter?

Hildegard and Erich Moser in 1951

Iris Johnson was a girl of eleven living in Oswaldtwistle, Lancashire, when the Second World War ended. Over a year later, one of her relations came into contact with some German prisoners who were part of a working party from the nearby POW camp. When Iris's mother heard that prisoners were allowed to visit private homes, she invited three of the men to tea on Christmas Day, hoping someone would have shown similar kindness to British lads imprisoned in Germany. The men met the family, Mr and Mrs Johnson, Iris (just 13) and Elsie (4). At the end of the day, Iris's father said to the men, "If you are this way again, feel free to call in."

One of the men, Erich Moser, aged twenty-two, sought out the family two weeks later. He recognised their house by the clothes brushes which he could just see hanging on the wall in the entrance hall. He said – perhaps as an excuse – that he had lost a cigarette lighter and wondered if he had left it at the house. From then on he visited the family most Saturdays. Understanding some English, he kept asking people to speak more slowly to help him. Some months later he was moved to a camp near Preston, fifteen miles away, but he continued to visit the family at weekends. However, when he was moved farther south before being repatriated, they lost touch with him. Having no way of contacting him, they felt they would probably never see their German friend again.

In 1951, out of the blue, Mr and Mrs Johnson received an engagement card from Erich: he was to be married to Hildegard Klaiber. The couple went to live in Weisenbach on the edge of the Black Forest, where the bride's father was the Bürgermeister. Hildegard turned out to be an extremely good letter-writer and a pen-friendship was established. In time, pictures of their baby Veronika were sent across the sea to England

Some of the many cards and letters written by Hildegard Moser to the English friends she has never seen

and news of family occasions such as Hildegard's parents' silver wedding in 1954. Gifts also were exchanged: Iris remembers receiving dolls dressed in German costumes. Her sister Elsie was sent a pink handkerchief case and a wooden bowl which depicted a lovely scene from the Black Forest was sent to their parents.

When Iris married Alan Gardner, a standing invitation was issued by Erich and Hildegard to go to visit them in Germany. In 1959 they made plans to take up this kind offer, but as Iris became pregnant the trip was cancelled. After their daughter Lesley was born in 1960, a white baby dress and coat arrived from Germany with three coloured bands at the bottom, in lemon, pink and blue. A cardigan was received on the birth of their second daughter, Alison, seven years later.

Over the next thirty years, letters, cards and occasional gifts were sent in both directions, especially at times of family events. In May 1975 there was rejoicing at Veronika's marriage, but two months later came the sad news of Erich's death, at only 50 years of age. The memorial card said he had been very happy at his work, but people believed he worked too hard: he died of heart failure. By coincidence Iris's husband died at the same age from a similar cause nine years later.

Eventually Iris received messages not only from Hildegard but also from her son Herbert, his wife Marita and their children Melanie and Tina, as well as from Veronika, husband Kurt and son Andreas. On a card at Christmas 1990 were the words, "Maybe we shall see each other soon." Then at Christmas 1991 Iris was very surprised to receive a telephone call from Veronika in Germany, saying that they were hoping to come to England the following July. She, her husband and their son would all come with her mother, Erich's widow, Hildegard. This was to be a big event, but it did not happen. In May, Veronika wrote to say she herself had health problems and the visit was called off.

Hildegard Moser (middle) in August 1989 with her daughter Veronika, her son Herbert and her three grandchildren, Andreas, Melanie and Tina

Over fifty years after that first lost cigarette lighter, Iris treasured the letters and cards from her German friends. She still possessed the wooden bowl from the Black Forest, and her sister Elsie had kept safe the pink handkerchief case. In January 2001 Iris Gardener died unexpectedly. It seems the pen-friends were destined never to meet.

Post Script. In the year following Iris's death, her daughter Alison, with her husband Steve and their daughter Chloé, went to visit Veronika and her family in Weisenbach. Everyone they met in Germany was very welcoming, friendly and generous with their hospitality. The visit was a

great success and was even reported in the local newspaper. They watched a video recording together of the German TV documentary, *Wie aus Feinden Freunde werden* (How Enemies Became Friends), based on the present author's book, *Enemies Become Friends*. The story touched their hearts, and they were all pleased to see Iris feature in the programme shortly before her death.

At last, the two families have come together. Iris and Erich would be pleased.

Iris Gardner in 1999 with treasured letters, cards, gifts and photographs from her German pen-friends

24. Love Finds a Way

Peter Roth lived in the village of Erbach, 30 miles south east of Frankfurt-am-Main in Germany. He had been an unruly child ever since he realised that his mother, who died in 1921 when he was only two, would never come back. Because he felt that everyone was against him, he rebelled against authority, this attitude staying with him until much later in life. People tried using force to make him obedient, but the more he was beaten the worse he seemed to become. The only school record he held was that of most caned boy. Fortunately he had a loving stepmother, who prevented his father from seeing his school reports, but sadly he could never bring himself to show her any affection, something he always regretted.

As a young man, Peter fought in the German infantry before being captured in 1944 in Normandy by Canadians and brought to England as a prisoner of war. After being moved through several camps in the north and south of the country he arrived at Friday Bridge, a village between March and Wisbech in Cambridgeshire. In February 1945, he was sent under guard on a working party to Floods Ferry Farm near the village of Benwick on the other side of March. His job was to dig up carrots, and on principle he did as little work as possible. Perhaps because his name was an easy one for the English guards to say, or perhaps because he would not willingly cooperate, Peter felt he was often picked upon.

Making Friends

One day three men were needed to use a riddling machine to sift and sort the carrots, to bag the best ones for market. Peter was chosen for this work and given the hardest job, turning the handle to operate the machine. When they ran out of bags, Peter was the one told to go across the road to get empty bags from another working party riddling potatoes. This group was not of German prisoners but composed of three Italians, three British men and three young women. In true German fashion Peter went up to each of them in turn and shook hands, much to their surprise.

The following day, during the lunch break, Peter decided to try to pay another visit to this group across the road. The guards that day were Irish and, in Peter's opinion, "more relaxed". When they settled down with their food, Peter made a bold dash over the road with his bread and cheese in his hand. At first he hid behind a large potato clamp, a long heap of earth covering tons of potatoes kept there over winter from the previous harvest. From this hiding place he saw to his astonishment that everyone, except two of the women, went to the nearby farmhouse for their lunch break. Peter emerged from the clamp, which then successfully hid him from the road, and tried to speak to the women, but neither spoke German nor French. He noticed that their lunch was beetroot, lettuce and bread and concluded they had less to eat than he did.

That evening Peter stripped his hut's garden of all its flowers, six snowdrops. Next day he presented the tiny bouquet to one of the women, Margaret, who was unmarried. In return she gave him a cigarette and a piece of cake. Every day Peter weighed up the risk of dashing across the road at lunch time, depending on which guards were on duty. Determined to help his newfound friends, he went without his own corned beef ration until he had enough to present to Margaret in an open tin. She declined the gift saying they had enough to eat, but, as Peter persisted, she eventually took the tin. Some time later Peter learnt what happened to it. Hearing where it had come from, Margaret's mother was suspicious and decided to try it out on the cat. The cat took a sniff but would not eat it, and the hard won meat ended up in the dustbin.

Peter was very attracted by Margaret so he decided to make her a special cigarette case expressing his feelings. He already had tools for the task, a knife made out of a piece of iron from his bed in a previous camp and a needle made from a sardine tin opener. His third tool was a razor blade. Using a piece of mahogany, he carved on the lid his name and Margaret's, the rising sun inside a heart, and a border of barbed wire. Inside the cigarette case he embroidered a wild rose with wool from the edge of a blanket. Margaret was so taken aback by such an unexpected and wonderful gift that she did not know what to say, but, as Peter now remarks, he wouldn't have understood it anyway (see colour photographs)!

From then onwards Peter saw Margaret briefly most working days. At 2:30 pm she would set off on her bicycle to travel home to March, passing where Peter was working. A discreet short encounter would enable him to pass a note requesting an item such as glue, and she would give him scraps of material which he could use to make toys. He bartered the toys to obtain toiletries and other small luxuries. Peter must indeed have had a talent for making things with his improvised tools. On one occasion he carved a complete chess set of 32 figures, working every spare minute on them, though he never received any payment. Looking back on it later, he is baffled as to how he managed such a task.

By this time, Peter understood some English but could barely speak it. Mr Johnson, the farmer who owned Floods Ferry Farm and other land in the area, asked Peter if he would concrete the farmyard. Unfortunately this led to an unforeseen sequence of events. The man who operated the concrete mixer saw that Margaret was friendly with a German prisoner. He threatened to make this known in the town of March, where Margaret lived with the farmer's mother, which might have harmed the farmer's reputation. To prevent this happening the farmer asked a friend, a fruit-grower ten miles away in Wisbech, to put in a request to the camp for Peter to work on *his* farm as a tree pruning specialist. Peter had no knowledge of all this nor of the undesirable changes which were to come about, neither was he a pruning specialist. Back at camp he was therefore surprised to be summoned to the German commandant responsible for allocating POW labour to farmers and told to start work in Wisbech for the fruit-grower, Mr Hickman.

Peter was heartbroken at being parted from Margaret. He immediately set about trying to renew contact, but the war had not yet ended, and any such enterprise was risky. The camp interpreter, Dillman, was from a village near to Peter's own in Germany, so he persuaded him to translate his letter to Margaret into English. Then he asked a Swiss friend, Simmy, to deliver the letter and request a reply, though that was a dangerous mission. This happened several times: it cost Peter hundreds of cigarettes. He waited anxiously for the right reply and eventually received what he wanted, Margaret's promise to meet him outside the camp. She was probably unaware of the danger involved but knew enough not to tell anyone about it, nor even to ask advice, but she probably did not realise that an attempt at escape from a camp might be foiled by gunfire. As Peter recalls, "When I think of it now I don't know how I dared do it." Peter's plan was to get out of the camp by cutting the barbed wire, and to return again without being seen. The only time this might possibly be done was at the changing of the guard which happened every two hours, dark nights being easier than moonlit ones. Peter tested this several times with some success until he was ready to set up a meeting with Margaret. It worked: he was free for a while with a girl in his arms, and he was very pleased with himself, feeling he had thwarted authority. For a time Peter and Margaret met twice a week, and the escape route was never discovered.

On one memorable occasion, Peter got through to the finals of the camp chess championship, but the time of the match was unexpectedly changed from afternoon to evening, and he had no means of letting Margaret know he could not meet her that evening. The match began, but after a few moves Peter felt he must leave, so excused himself for a few minutes and went to keep his date. After his friends had searched for him unsuccessfully, he lost the match and the chance to become camp chess champion. The next day he had a lot of explaining to do: his excuse was that he had lost his nerve for the match.

Margaret Stratton's Influence

What sort of person was this young woman whom the uneducated boy from Erbach village had taken every opportunity to pursue? Margaret Stratton was an only child and perhaps a loner, who had found a measure of independence at an early age and had acquired many skills. Now she was a talented woman of thirty-two years of age, six years older than Peter, and well respected in the town. She was artistic, painting wedding photographs in oils before colour photographs were available, and supplied stores with some of her handiwork, such as flowers made out of glitter wax and dolls which she had dressed. She was a performer on stage, singing, tap-dancing, acting and producing concert parties. She was also adept at tennis, swimming and skating. Peter described her in retrospect as an innocent young woman regarded as "untouchable" by the young men of the town.

Shortly after the war ended, Peter was moved to a small camp in Manea, south east of March. His problem once again was how to contact Margaret. One day, as he was jumping off a lorry in the village, he suddenly saw her quite unexpectedly in the street, as she happened to be visiting this very village as producer of a concert party due to perform in the village hall. Naturally Peter was keen to arrange to meet her and used sign language to point out a meeting place and time. That evening, not knowing the area well, he trampled through hedges and dykes, hid in bushes, was frightened by a horse and spotted by a group of youths, but had to return to the camp without seeing Margaret and with his POW uniform torn. Minutes after he had arrived back at his hut, guards burst in. They were carrying out an unexpected roll call of the camp, perhaps because of information from the group of youths, but Peter had arrived back just in time.

As Christmas 1945 approached, Margaret wanted Peter to spend Christmas Day at her home. She and her mother lived at "Elmwood", a large house in March occupied by Farmer Johnson's mother and her staff. Margaret's mother was cook and in charge of the servants, living in one section of the house. Although the war was over, prisoners were not yet allowed into private homes, and there was no official way of organising such a visit, but it was thrilling to Peter to try to outwit authority again. A taxi driver, Douglas Fiddieng, risked the reputation of his business by taking Peter the ten-mile journey to March and through the centre of the town on Christmas morning and back again in the evening. He also lent Peter some of his own clothes for the day. Peter was dropped at the house's back entrance, used by the servants, and if anyone saw the stranger he was simply "Margaret's boyfriend". Mrs Johnson was unaware she had a German under her roof in the other part of the house. Margaret paid the taxi driver 13 shillings for this help, and her mother gave him half a pound of farm butter, a luxury at this time. Margaret also promised, "If we ever get married, Douglas, you shall take us to the church." After a wonderful Christmas feast provided by Margaret and her mother, Peter congratulated himself that he had once again outmanoeuvred the establishment.

Years later he heard the true story. Police Sergeant Green had been tipped off and given Peter's exact movements by one of Mrs Johnson's maids, but he had turned a blind eye. Why? Because Margaret had worked hard in the past to raise money to support British soldiers, taking part in concerts after a hard day's farm work. Sergeant Green told Peter, "I could not harm that good girl. Her only sin was falling in love. With a clear conscience I made sure you had a chance."

All German prisoners were interviewed individually, assessed and classified, so that decisions could be made about where they should be held and when they were to be repatriated. Peter was asked if he had been part of the Hitler Youth movement, and what was his view of the Polish "corridor". His grade was then recorded as "A", no Nazi tendencies, which meant he might be repatriated soon. This posed him with a problem, so he quickly asked the officer if there was a chance to stay longer in England. Needing a reason, he said, "I have nothing to hide, only that I love a young lady whom I intend to make my wife". Peter was re-graded as "B+" to give him more time in Britain after which the

rules about not staying here were relaxed. For a further two years, Peter's time as a prisoner was full of escapades and excitement. In fact, looking back on it all from the age of 80, he says "My life has had never a dull moment."

In the light summer months it was impossible to get in and out of the camp without being seen. Instead communication was by letter. Margaret gave Peter a sheet of stamps. Peter took these – and the writing paper, needle, new pocket knife, money and other secret belongings – and in a neat packet buried them under a hedge. His most prized possession was a photograph of Margaret which he had framed with some difficulty in part of

Picture of Margaret Stratton preserved in a tin, said to have saved Peter Roth from doing many foolish things

an old insecticide tin. Peter now says that looking at Margaret's photo-graph in its tin frame prevented him from doing many foolish things, such as planning daring escapes. He felt he must not do anything to hurt or sadden her. His attitude to the English changed and to life itself. From the "unruly boy" of Erbach village he gradually became a law-abiding member of society. "This is what a picture did to me!" Peter recalls. The photograph in the tin frame, which was always either with him or buried for safety, seemed to alter his character.

When the fishing season started Peter was summoned to see the British guard. One of the guards had been looking for worms and had come upon Peter's packet. "You are the only Peter in this camp. Do these things belong to you?" he was asked. Always quick thinking, Peter invented what he now calls "a white lie to save my bacon". He responded that he had found the stamps on the pavement. They were a stamp collector's dream: he wanted to take them home as a souvenir from England but had hidden them because he knew he should not have them. His tale was believed, but the guard regretted that he could not let Peter keep the unused stamps. He would send them to his wife who would use them to write to him, and he would then bring the used stamps to Peter for his collection. Then there was the pocket knife which had superseded the crude one made in a previous camp. How had he obtained that? Peter replied, "Sorry, sir, I cannot reveal who gave it to me as I do not want to get anyone else into trouble, as it was one of your own mates." After more questions he divulged that the guard's predecessor had given him the knife to use to make a rocking horse for Christmas for his son. The guard was moved by this story and allowed Peter to keep everything except the stamps.

Despite the white lie, a relationship was struck between the guard and Peter. True to his word the guard later brought the used stamps and other stamps for Peter's supposed collection. Peter made a toy for the guard's daughter, four birds pecking from a plate, moved by a swinging weight under the handle, to prove that the knife was used for nothing more sinister than carving toys.

The very severe winter of early 1947 was to provide extra opportun-ities to see Margaret, but with it came more trouble. Peter was working on a smallholding laying a concrete floor in a barn. The weather was too cold for making concrete so the job had to be postponed. The driver of the vehicle which normally took Peter to work was bribed with 20 cigarettes to drop Peter at March instead of at his workplace. On arrival, Peter consumed a large meal of home-made sausages and spent some hours with Margaret and her mother. He returned to camp by bicycle laden with pork and sausages for his friends. These visits happened for several days. At the end of the week, Peter went to the smallholding to have his timesheet signed, without realising that the adverse weather conditions had led to all usual work being stopped. He was the only prisoner going out to work each morning. Peter tried to cover his tracks by getting people to lie for him, but the result was solitary confinement. He spent the first night pacing up and down the 12 foot by 5 foot cell trying to make up a credible story. When he was summoned to see the commandant, the sergeant did a good job of removing Peter's hat, taking a handful of hair as well, though he had little enough to begin with. Peter spun his tale. The commandant considered it for a few moments and then declared, "I do not believe one word of it," and gave him 14 days' detention. However, those two weeks in the "calaboose" were an experience Peter would not have wanted to miss. He had more to eat, more cigarettes, more help from friends and did more bribing of guards than at any other time. By many he was looked upon as a hero, he had broken the rules.

A Free Man

At last Peter's repatriation date was decided, 5 November 1947. He informed his father and stepmother that he wanted to stay in Britain and marry an Englishwoman, though they were not pleased. Here was a dilemma, whether to forsake his beloved Germany and his home, where he had a house and land, or to stay here where he had the love of a girl. There was no contest: he must stay. Now Peter realises this was "a big, big gamble, the biggest I ever took in my life".

On being released, Peter had few possessions, just a jacket and trousers with POW patches on them. He got work on the land for £4.10 shillings a week. His attitude to authority had changed. He felt he "had to prove that not all Germans are bad". After taking the moment-ous decision to stay in this country, making friends was the next task. By avoiding subjects such as politics, religion and the royal family, he tried never to provoke people.

By Christmas 1947 Peter had saved enough money to buy Mar-garet a ring. In the following spring there was a sensation in the market town of March when the respected and talented Margaret was to marry a former prisoner. It had taken a German prisoner to "take her off her

Margaret and Peter – Early Days

pedestal", as Peter puts it. This was the first wedding the town had seen between an ex-German prisoner and a local woman, and Douglas Fiddieng provided the taxi to church, his reward for risking the name of his business at Christmas 1945.

Love overcomes all hurdles, and soon Peter no longer felt a stranger. For this he is grateful to the English people for

Margaret and Peter in 1999 with some of Peter's carvings from his POW days

treating him with fairness and friendship. In 1951, Farmer Johnson lent him money for a year to buy a piece of land for a nursery. There was no written agreement, just a handshake. He repaid it as promised, and as no interest was requested he gave the farm gardener 500 tulip bulbs, though the farmer's wife never knew where they had come from. Now, over 50 years later, Peter and Margaret are still in contact with Mr and Mrs Johnson's daughter, Ann.

In later years, after moving to nearby Peterborough, Peter became involved with the Anglo-German Club and with the town twinning scheme with Viersen near Düsseldorf. He is proud to have mixed with a cross-section of the British community, from elderly widows who brought their ailing plants to be revived in his nursery, to artists, aristocrats and Members of Parliament. At international events he welcomes guests in French, Spanish and German, no mean task, as he puts it, for an uneducated village lad. Margaret, of course, has continued her many interests. Her floral art has been exhibited in Peterborough and in Ely Cathedral, both young students and adults benefiting from her teaching of art. Her proudest moments have been when for six years she had the chief position of hosting royalty at the East of England Show.

The story draws to its close with Peter's own words.

In 1950 we were blessed with a little daughter. Now we have two grown-up lovely grand-children and a beautiful little great-granddaughter. We worked very hard, shared all in our life. We own our own house and car, but most of all each other . . . . I still love my original home, and I love Germany, but I am contented where I am. We are as happy as we were all those long years ago. Love found its way.

25. Friendships Despite the Bombs

Surely it is unlikely that people who were bombed during the war would want to make friends with the enemy. The story of Long Ashton seems to contradict this assumption.

Long Ashton, south of Bristol docks, was on the flight path of German bombers on their way to demolish shipping. The planes crossed reservoirs where unfortunately the moon was often reflected on the water. In addition beacons were lit in the area to deceive the bombers into dropping their loads too soon, with the result that Long Ashton and nearby Bedminster received blastings out of all proportion to their importance, beginning in the early years of the war.

Rev. Hugh Knapman, the vicar of Long Ashton, was in his study one evening talking on the telephone to his doctor. His mother was in another room. Looking out of the bay window, he could see the crater left by a 500-pound bomb which had fallen three weeks earlier in the field adjacent to the vicarage. The roof of his church also had received bomb damage, and the belfry had been set alight in another raid. Suddenly, at seven o'clock, without any warning, a bomb fell outside the study window, shattering it to smithereens and blowing the vicar from the study to the hall. The doctor heard the explosion on the other end of the telephone line and thought they had all been killed. Although the vicarage and outbuildings were left in ruins, miraculously the vicar and his mother were unhurt.

The morning after the bomb. The vicar's mother, the curate, and the sexton standing in a crater, head just visible at the front of the picture

They were more fortunate than many people in the area, where there were many casualties during the war. In fact, local people were not the only ones to meet their death in Long Ashton. On the night of 23 November 1944 seven Polish airmen and their Halifax bomber crashed into the field by the church. Over 50 years later a memorial to those men was placed in the churchyard wall, listing their names and ranks and ending, "They died far from their homeland in defence of freedom".

At the end of the war, Bedminster Camp was opened in the vicinity, housing about 2,000 German prisoners. Many of the men were from the German air force, and some had themselves been responsible for dropping bombs in the area including the one on the vicarage. It was not very likely these prisoners would be welcome in Long Ashton!

Their Lutheran pastor, also a prisoner, Pastor Walter Krauss, approached Rev. Hugh Knapman in summer 1946 reporting that some of the prisoners would like to join in the services at the church. Here was a dilemma for the vicar: what should his response be? He recalls, "There were naturally high feelings against Germans, but I put it to the parish, and the men were invited to morning service," attending first on 4 August 1946. A German friend, Kurt Heldt, who had escaped from Germany before the war and settled in Long Ashton, helped to translate the vicar's sermon. Mr Knapman then delivered his message in English and German, although there seems to be some doubt as to whether the German version was perfectly understood! Addressing the congregation as God's children, he said that the Christian fellowship which bound them together was far deeper than that of birth or of race. On several other occasions the prisoners attended services at the church and gradually began to make friends with local people.

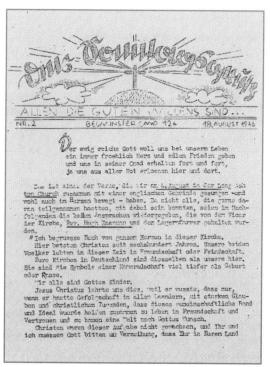

"Sonntagsgruss" (Sunday Newsletter), quoting the vicar's sermon, 18 August 1946

One Sunday afternoon two POWs went the from house to house in Long Ashton trying to sell items they had made. One resident, Arthur Newman, was particularly attracted by a ten-inch-wide photograph stand. It had two sheets of glass held by two dogs carved

Heinz, Barbara, Hein and Janet in 1946

beautifully in wood. He bought it for his 22-year-old daughter Audrey. Over 50 years later, Audrey still has the stand in use (see colour photographs).

Another couple, Harry and Ethel Randall, hearing on the wireless that prisoners could be invited into homes, immediately sent their son-in-law, Wilfred Mitchell, to the camp to invite one to Sunday tea. He came back with two, Albert and Hein. Albert had been a postman at home, a married man with a daughter: Hein was of South African origin. From then on the two men visited their newfound friends most Sundays, sometimes accompanied by another prisoner, Heinz, whose great desire was to return home and marry someone very rich! Over 50 years later, Mr and Mrs Randall's daughter, Ivy Mitchell, recalls these details. The men made many presents for the family. One was an oval shopping basket for Mrs Randall, woven from willows collected from the hedgerows. With a small knife, they carved toys for Ivy and Wilfred's daughter Janet, such as two dolls which danced and rotated as they were pushed along. Janet still has a ship in a bottle made by one of the prisoners and named "Barbara" after her aunt.

Such friendships seemed to grow up naturally in the Long Ashton area, despite the havoc and destruction caused there by the war. They were valued greatly and remembered for many years. One friendship led to a reunion of the two clergymen three decades later. A local couple, Paul and Ina Tubb, had invited prisoners to Sunday lunch and had struck up a particular friendship with the Lutheran pastor, Walter Krauss. Almost exactly 30 years later, on 11 June 1976, an unplanned reunion took place. By this time the erstwhile Vicar of Long Ashton, Hugh Knapman, and

Letter from Pastor Krauss 30
years later, 19 August 1976

his wife Sonia, were retired and living in a village in Somerset. However, Mr and Mrs Tubb sought them out and brought visitors to their door. The visitors were Pastor Krauss and his granddaughter Ursula, from Hüssingen in Germany. A lively conversation ensued, dispelling the mists of the intervening years. Photographs were taken including some on Mr Knapman's new instant camera, a novelty in those days. Mr Tubb recorded the animated conversation on tape, so that Pastor Krauss could relive the meeting when he was back home in Germany. The barking of the dog could also be heard on the tape in the background!

Later that year Rev. and Mrs Knapman received a letter from Pastor Krauss. He had enclosed a snap taken during the visit and an old copy of the Bedminster Camp's "Sonntagsgruss" (Sunday Newsletter) for 18 August 1946, quoting the vicar's memorable sermon.

The letter read:

Hüssingen, 19.8.76

Dear Friends,

Nearly ten weeks went away since the lovely day we met again after exactly thirty years. Thank you so much for all your kindness, we shall never forget. The added snap may be helpful for you in some way to brush up the reminiscence.

Paul Tubb has kept our conversation and clinking of glasses on his recorder. To my birthday my family presented me a "Tonbandgerät" [tape recorder]. So I am enabled to listen to your voices and last but not least the barking of your clever dog. It is very pretty, isn't it? Hoping you all are very well, we remain

Yours sincerely,

Ursula and Walter Krauss.

As a tangible reminder of friendship despite the bombs, these documents have been carefully preserved by Rev. and Mrs Knapman into the next century.

26. The Friendly Bürgermeister

Clemens Schwertmann, a building engineer and architect, was Bürgermeister (or mayor) of his home-town, Melle in Germany, for over 26 years, from May 1970 to November 1996. Melle, a town of 47,000 inhabitants, lies near Osnabrück in the north of the country.

On becoming mayor, he started to carry out a plan of action about which he was passionate. He believed profoundly in the importance of friendship between nations, especially between people who had been enemies. He decided to encourage such relationships by setting up partnerships between Melle and towns in other countries, in eastern and western Europe, in the USA and in Britain.

As soon as he took up office, Mayor Schwertmann established a link with British soldiers from the garrison at Osnabrück. This led during the 1970s to visits to Melle town hall, first from representatives of the Queen's Lancashire Regiment, then from the Argyll and Sutherland Highlanders and even a visit from the British Major-General O.M. Roome, Chief of the Joint Services Liaison Organisation in Bonn. In 1973 Mayor Schwertmann, accompanied by his wife Anneliese and their son Christoph, travelled to Lancashire to visit the Regimental Headquarters of the Queen's Lancashire Regiment in Warrington where they were

Reception in Melle for The Argyll and Sutherland Highlanders, January 1975

thanked for the kindness they had shown to the 1st Battalion during its term in Germany.

The mayor's next link was a twinning arrangement with the English town of Etwall, five miles southwest of Derby. It began in 1977 and has included a strong relationship between the John Port School in Etwall and the Gymnasium in Melle. Through this scheme many lifelong family relationships have been developed. At the time of writing, the celebration of the 25th anniversary of this partnership is being planned.

In fact, the friendly Bürgermeister established more than 15 official connections between his home-town of Melle and towns in other places and countries. These include Eeken in France; Gent, Eecke and Sint Denijs Westrem in Belgium; Eicken in Switzerland; Jekabpils in Latvia; Homyel in Belarus; Torcok in Russia; Nigde in Turkey; Bad Dürrenberg in East Germany; and Reinickendorf, a northern suburb of Berlin, as well as Etwall in England and New Melle in Missouri, USA.

At the inauguration of the American agreement, in June 1988, a group of 47 Germans travelled from Melle to New Melle, near St Louis in Missouri, for a six-day stay in private homes. New Melle is so called because Germans from Melle emigrated to the USA and settled there in the mid-1800s. For some of the Germans visiting in 1988 it was an opportunity to meet long lost relatives. For example, an American professor, Dr Walter Kamphoefner, who acted as interpreter, was one whose ancestors had come from Melle. When the German mayor signed the official partnership agreement with New Melle town officials, at a key ceremony, he took the opportunity to make a fluent speech in English as

Official of New Melle, Missouri signs the partnership
agreement with Melle, Germany, June 1988.
Mayor Clemens Schwertmann on left

well as to give an impromptu tune on his harmonica. The speech summed up the philosophy behind his passion. After a few jokes and the setting of the scene he explained some of his strongly held beliefs as follows.

The effect of the Second World War gave rise to a most important event and to one of the greatest moments in my life: enemies became friends . . . . The best ways to keep peace and to realise partnership, relationship and friendship are not only treaties and agreements between the national governments, but also, and in my opinion, more useful and more effective are meetings between people at the base. We all are called to get engaged and to work for this wonderful idea. We all can help to improve it . . . . When people heap together and go together they'll become friends, and they'll remain friends. And that is a very important point for the future, to give a feeling of security especially to our young people. When you have friends instead of rivals, you can make your way in the future free from care. The occasion of this significant meeting is therefore one of the best possibilities. Whatever happened in the past, and whatever shall happen in the future, we always should be wise enough to seek happiness not only in material values but in peace, friendship and love.

What was the reason for Herr Schwertmann's prolonged passion for developing such links, and what was one of the "greatest moments" in his life connected with the Second World War, to which he referred in his speech in New Melle? The answer to both these questions is the experience of three years spent as a prisoner of war in Britain between 1945 and 1948.

After harvesting potatoes in Okehampton and clearing up barbed wire in St Austell Bay, the 21-year-old Clemens Schwertmann was held in Plymouth for two and a half years where his job was laying concrete for new roads and foundations for new houses, along with about one hundred other prisoners. It was hard and tedious work. This tedium was relieved for Clemens when he met a local family, Mr and Mrs Donald Towell and their 14-year-old son, Gerald, mentioned elsewhere in this book. The family had lived through the devastation of the Plymouth blitz, but Mr Towell, who had served in the British navy, felt that hatred had gone too far: Germans were human beings too. For these views and for inviting POWs into his house, he and his family not surprisingly experienced antagonism from some of their neighbours who had lost relatives in the war.

Clemens was one of five prisoners befriended by the Towell family. The prisoners became wonderful comrades of the teenage Gerald, playing cards, going to the beach together and visiting the houses of his school friends, such as John Roppen, Barbara Congdon, Pat Riggs and Kev Park. Thus the prisoners extended their circle of acquaintances among

Clemens Schwertmann, Gerd Halbsgut
and Klaus Meyer, with Gerald Towell
at the front, ready for a swim at
Whitsands Bay, Cornwall, 1947

the population of Plymouth and Gerald gained a new friend. Together the young men went to watch the Plymouth Devils Speedway and Plymouth Argyle football team as well as to concerts, the theatre and the cinema.

Looking back on that era, Herr Schwertmann remembers thankfully this "unforgettable and exciting time" in a foreign land when he came to regard Gerald as a true friend and Mr and Mrs Towell as his "parents by proxy". They stood in for his own parents whom he had not seen for five years. He also remembers meeting "many, many good English people". These experiences made a deep and lasting impression on him.

From the other side of the friendship, Mr Gerald Towell, now living near Cheltenham, explains the influence this had on him as a teenage boy, with these words.

Wartime conditions and propaganda had led us to believe that all German soldiers were fanatical Nazis. Getting to know them was a revelation, and ever since I have not believed that the British are a superior race. I treat people as individuals and dislike it intensely when some people brand some nations as bad. It has taught me that the "little Englander" mentality is quite evil and stupid. These friendships have been a major influence in my life.

Clemens so greatly valued the warmth and esteem he had found with English people, that after repatriation in May 1948, he determined to do all he could in his life to bring about understanding between different peoples, especially between former enemies. He felt that to become acquainted with people of other nations, seeing families in their own homes and neighbourhoods, would bring respect, friendship, love and peace for the world.

His individual relationship with his "parents by proxy" and with their son Gerald continued of course, with numerous visits both ways between the families from 1948 until the present day, helped at first by the coincidence that Gerald was stationed not far from Melle with BAOR for his national service. In time, the wives and children of the two men were included in these visits. It

Anneliese Schwertmann, Gerald, Donald and Eileen Towell and Clemens Schwertmann in England, 1982

was during one of the town twinning visits to Etwall, in 1987, that Clemens went to see his "parents by proxy" for the last time before their deaths, which he recalls with sadness.

In May 1998, on one of Clemens and Anneliese Schwertmann's visits to Gerald and Christine Towell's home near Cheltenham, they all travelled down to Plymouth to visit the site of the POW camp and remind themselves of those unusual times. It was exactly 50 years since Clemens had left Plymouth as a free man. Together they drove over some of the very concrete laid by Clemens and his comrades when they were making a new road in the northern outskirts of Plymouth. After half a century, the concrete was still in place: not surprising, one might say, as it was laid by a future building engineer and architect!

However, it is as the friendly Bürgermeister that the citizens of Melle, and the people of many other towns and countries, have reason to remember with gratitude and affection Herr Schwertmann, who has now had the worthy title of Honorary Mayor of Melle conferred upon him. The local newspaper celebrated his 75th birthday on 28 November 2000 with an article under the heading, "Bridges of Communication built through Encounters". It paid tribute to the way in which he had brought together people of many nationalities in a spirit of friendship, acknowledging that this achievement had its origin in personal friendships made during his time of captivity in England.

In his retirement, the Honorary Mayor of Melle can rest assured that his youthful dream for a growth in understanding and respect between peoples has influenced thousands of families in many nations, and has become a reality in their lives. He has played a significant part in working towards peace in the world.

27. The Oak Plaque

Alois Degurse emigrated from his home in Germany to America before the First World War. After his marriage, he and his American wife Mary settled near the town of Trinidad in southern Colorado near the foot of the Rocky Mountains, where they owned a sugar beet farm. There was a lot of hard work to be done on the farm, and all water had to be hauled some distance from Trinidad.

During the Second World War German prisoners were stationed in a camp nearby. Because Alois was German, and because more hands were needed on the farm, he and Mary were very pleased when it was arranged for men from the camp to come to the farm daily during the summer to help with the harvest. The prisoners had their own food supplies, but Mary used to supplement their rations with little extras such as pots of beans, because she appreciated their help and was sympathetic to their plight.

One of the prisoners had been a colonel in the German army so, due to his officer rank, he did none of the heavy work himself. Indeed he spent much of his time near the farmhouse playing with Paula, the young granddaughter of Alois and Mary. Even now Paula still has a distant memory of him. The Colonel whiled away many hours carving a piece of oak with a pocket knife. Eventually it was seen to be the head of Jesus wearing the crown of thorns.

A rapport built up between Alois, Mary, little Paula and the Colonel, partly because of the common language and background which he and Alois shared, and partly due to the long summer days he spent in the vicinity of the farmhouse. When the time came for the Colonel to leave, he unexpectedly, and to Mary's great delight, presented her with the carved and varnished plaque of Christ's head, created with patience and skill (see colour photographs).

Mary and Alois admired the plaque for many years, keeping it carefully as a memento of the Colonel and as a reminder of that wartime summer when German prisoners of war shared the harvesting of the sugar beet. Eventually Mary gave it to her son Paul who in turn passed it on to his son Darrel, of Madison, Wisconsin, in whose possession it remains treasured to this day.

28. The Extraordinary Friendship

Fritz Defèr was only fourteen when the war started. He and his school mates in Dresden hardly thought they would be taking part in any fighting: it would all be over soon. But before he was eighteen, Fritz was called up into the German army and within a year he was captured in Normandy. His first task, in July 1944, was to dig graves for corpses brought from surrounding battlefields, not a very auspicious beginning to what was to be a three-and-a-half-year stretch as a prisoner of war.

Life in Britain

Soon he was moved to Britain, and fortunately for Fritz he already had an interest in the country, having studied English for nearly seven years at Dresden Grammar School. His father had a liking for English literature and a fondness for Charles Dickens in particular, so Fritz had grown up knowing about the characters of *David Copperfield, Mr Micawber* and *Uriah Heep.* English literature had given him some understanding of the country's history, tradition and customs as well as a feel for the language. The adventure on which he was about to start, as a prisoner of war, was to take him to many parts of Britain, from Edinburgh to Essex and Cambridge to Cornwall, enabling him to obtain a first-hand knowledge of the country. He was an alert young man, keen to "grip all chances offered", as he now puts it.

Fritz Defèr as a POW in early 1947 aged 21

Of most concern to Fritz was that he had no news of his parents and younger brother. After being moved from Edinburgh to a camp near Durham, he was alarmed to read in the *Daily Mail* about the raid of 13 February 1945 on Dresden. As his home-town of Freital bordered on Dresden he was naturally extremely worried for the safety of his family.

Two months later he at last received two letters from his parents, but he soon saw they had been written in January, before the Dresden raid. Unfortunately Fritz had to wait until the following January for the delivery of the next letter from home. Meanwhile he himself sent written messages to Freital though he discovered later that only two of them reached his parents before the end of 1945. These delays were no doubt due first to the war itself and then perhaps to the initial confusion after the splitting of Germany into administrative zones, Dresden becoming part of the Russian Zone. However, from 1946 Fritz and his family were able to exchange mail more easily. Indeed, when he was repatriated in November 1947 he found that his father had kept all his letters from Britain and had carefully numbered them 1 to 88!

Fritz was given many different kinds of work in Britain. He was a farm labourer in both the North East and Essex, he laid concrete bases for camp huts near Durham, and he broke up concrete slabs as part of the process of dismantling an anti-aircraft base in Devon. He dug trenches for a sewer system in Berkshire and was a clerk in the camp office in Plymouth.

He particularly liked his job near the camp in Bridestowe in Devon. He worked as a sign-writer at a military engineering depot in Tavistock. Each morning he was given sheets of amendments such as ". . . flue-lids, small: cancel number x-y/509 and substitute y-x/9905 . . ." Armed with a pot of white paint and a little hair brush he would search for the relevant items to alter the numbers as instructed. In this depot were numerous small parts for kitchen ranges, and Fritz added to his English vocabulary many technical terms for which he did not know the German equivalent. Here he worked with British tradesmen and soon became acquainted with a Mr William Baker, a man much older than himself, but with whom he seemed to share many interests and ideas. Mr Baker lent him English books, one day producing his own four stanza verse which he called "Summertime". Written in pencil on the back of a list it began:

> Thro' the beautiful summer days
> Roses and lilies grow sublime.
> With the glorious summer rays
> Every flower seems to shine.

The poem went on to tell of waving rye, gorgeous butterflies, humming bees, singing birds, cows wading through a stream and other wonderful "works of nature revealed by the Creator's hand". Fritz felt that this poem reflected well their work surroundings: the depot consisted of a few huts on an area of uncultivated heath land adjacent to meadows. He translated the text of the poem into German, which seemed to please Mr Baker. They were both sorry when they had to part. However, Fritz had yet to meet the English person who was to become his lifelong friend.

1946 Poem by Mr William Baker, with Fritz Defèr's German translation

A Welcome Discovery

It was early in the winter of 1944 in the camp near the village of Crook near Durham, that Fritz made his best discovery about POW camps. This was a camp set among hilly countryside, covered by snow at the time, where the men had much fun sliding down slopes sitting on their tin plates. In this camp, and in all the ten or more later camps in which he stayed, Fritz found a quantity of books which could be borrowed. The number varied from camp to camp, but in the bigger camps there were "fairly voluminous libraries". Much of this literature was supplied by the YMCA, and the German books were mainly Swiss publications by authors whose works had been removed from German libraries during the Nazi era. Fritz discovered works by Thomas and Heinrich Mann, Georg Büchner, Stefan Zweig and Hermann Hesse, for example. He also read German translations of foreign literature including novels, poems and many works previously unknown to him. Fifty-five years later he is moved to describe this provision of books for POWs as follows. "This was a tremendous blessing for us. I cannot over-praise this benefit and still feel thankful for it. Not only that our minds were kept from fretting about our situation; they were broadened in many ways. Among them I found quite a lot written by authors whom I did not know, because they had been sorted out of public libraries in Nazi Germany. And during those three and a half years of my involuntary stay in Britain I was able to accumulate a wide knowledge of significant literary works which later helped me much in studying and subsequently teaching German and English language and literature." In one camp Fritz had time for reading as he and a friend were the only two German sentries. He spent many a night on sentry duty reading books. He remembers being able to obtain only volume two of Tolstoy's *War and Peace* because someone had always borrowed volume one!

In a small camp in Wadebridge in Cornwall Fritz started his "career" as an interpreter, working in the camp office. One of his tasks was to compile lists of the locations where prisoners were working in the community in small groups of between two and a dozen. The real situation differed from the official lists because the camp commander responded to private requests. When the colonel arrived to inspect the arrangements he sometimes found the wrong number of men working in some areas. Fritz remembers the ingenious ways in which the commander managed to dispel any doubts. If nothing else would work he engaged the colonel in conversation about dogs' ailments, in which both men were particularly interested. By overhearing all this, Fritz managed to improve his English. Perhaps the medical terms used about dogs were of some use when, as interpreter, he accompanied sick comrades to the doctor's surgery! Fortunately he had a dictionary to help with unknown terminology.

As well as hearing specialist vocabulary, Fritz also had to cope with strange idioms and local dialects from various parts of the country, some of which he now refers to as "vocabulary of a lower level". He therefore relished the sermons of the vicar at a parish church in Cornwall when, stationed at Consols Mine Camp in Par, the men were permitted to attend church services. Fritz found the vicar to be a very thoughtful and broad-minded man. It was a pleasure to listen to the "refined English" of his sermons and conversation.

One of Fritz's most interesting experiences brought him trouble after his return home. He was lucky enough to be selected to attend a six-week course at Wilton Park Training Centre in Beaconsfield, Buckinghamshire in the autumn of 1946. There he heard lectures on a wide range of subjects by excellent tutors and visiting personalities. The subjects included: German history since Bismarck, especially economy and home policy; citizen and state, constitutions of main countries, present problems of democracy; International relations, League of Nations and United Nations Organisation; Life in Britain, its history, traditions, establishments and today's problems. Visiting lecturers included Barbara Ward, editor of *The Economist* and member of the board of the BBC; Lord Beveridge who spoke about British democracy; and Dr Heinz Köppler, who was a lecturer in History at Oxford and also Principal of Wilton Park Training Centre. Every session was open for questions, and the students were encouraged to discuss the issues and state their own opinions.

After returning to the camp which sent him on this course, Fritz wrote an article on his experiences at Wilton Park, expressing his delight at what he had found there. This was published in the *Lagerzeitung*, the camp newspaper. Years later the authorities in the Russian Zone of Germany found out about Fritz's participation in this event and made trouble for him because of it. As he puts it, "Some officious people took it extremely amiss that I had been to that training centre and bothered me with awful suspicion."

A Friendship Begins
Not long after he attended this course the most momentous experiences of Fritz's life in Britain were to start. At the end of November 1946 the Devon camp was transferred from Bridestowe to the centre of Plymouth, a city which had suffered severe destruction from air raids in the war. Despite this, invitations were received at the camp for prisoners to share Christmas Day with local people. Fritz and a comrade were invited to the home of Mr Donald Towell of Devonport on the outskirts of Plymouth, where many houses had been bombed. After two and a half years as prisoners of war they were to enter a private home for the first time. Donald and his son, Gerald, aged fourteen and a half, met the men at the camp gates, and they all walked back to their house together. There the visitors were introduced to Donald's wife, Eileen, their large Alsatian called Bruno, and a lady who lodged with them. They were made very welcome, and the dog made the most of the occasion! However, after such a long time out of normal society it was not easy at first for the men to behave in a normal fashion. Fritz remembers sitting on the settee in front of the fire, having a little trouble balancing his cup and saucer.

They were puzzled by some of the English customs, paper hats, making a wish with the turkey "wishbone", the plum pudding ablaze and biting into a silver sixpence! In Germany the main celebration is on the night before Christmas, when candles are lit on Christmas trees, bearing coloured glass balls, red apples and chocolates. Goose is the traditional meat, and many different kinds of biscuits and gingerbread are eaten. Santa Claus has his day on 6 December when children's shoes, if clean enough, are filled in the night with sweets, nuts and oranges. It was talking about these different customs that helped the hosts and the visitors to start to get to know each other. The men were impressed when the lady lodger, whose husband had been killed in the war, gave them some sweets as a present. They all had a wonderful day together, and the men were invited to return the following afternoon.

It was from December 1946 that prisoners of war were more free to explore their surroundings, being allowed to walk within a five-mile radius of the camp. Not long afterwards they were permitted to enter public buildings and go to football matches. Fritz took the opportunities which presented themselves in Plymouth, a city and a port. He visited the city museum, the docks, the cinema and Plymouth Argyle football matches. But most of his spare time was spent with the Towell family. One weekend he and his friend did not visit the family, thinking they were taking up too much of their time, but Fritz remembers being scolded for it.

Donald Towell had been in the Navy since 1922, his last ship being the *Orion,* but now he was based in Plymouth in the Dockyard Police. He often helped with the preparation of the Sunday dinner when the Germans were visiting. Food was still rationed and sometimes there were electricity cuts, and Fritz remembers with pleasure Mr Towell's potatoes baked by the fire. He was of a calm and well-balanced nature, something of a contrast to his wife, Eileen. She is remembered by Fritz as a high-spirited, jolly woman who often made them all laugh. Everything was done to make the visitors feel at home, and she even acted as a mother to the young-looking Fritz. To complete the family, as well as Bruno the dog, there was Smoky the cat and a tortoise which had just come out of hibernation.

Fritz soon discovered that, although Gerald Towell was only fourteen and a half, and he was 21, the two young men shared many interests. Together they strolled over Plymouth Hoe where Gerald told Fritz about Sir Francis Drake and the Pilgrim Fathers. During Fritz's enforced time away from home he found Beethoven, Mozart and Bach strongly comforting. Imagine his surprise when he discovered that Gerald's favourite subject was music, and his great love was not popular or jazz but classical. Gerald loved nothing better than to show Fritz a new record he had obtained and to listen to it with him. On one occasion they exchanged landscapes: Gerald described a scene in the Scottish Highlands which he had visited, and Fritz told him about the Saxon sandstone hills along the River Elbe south of Dresden. Looking back, Fritz now sums up the friendship in these words, "Notwithstanding a gap of six and a half years between us, our relationship became more and more intimate, and the seeds were planted of a lifelong friendship." Circumstances dictated, though, that it was to be 45 years before each of them was able to show the other the landscapes they had described.

There was, in fact, a period of only three months when this friendship could develop face to face. In March 1947 Fritz was moved to a camp at St Columb Major in Cornwall, and the Towell family became friends with other prisoners from the Plymouth camp. Nevertheless they did not forget Fritz and made a date to go to see him in Cornwall, but before that happened he was moved to Pangbourne near Reading. Subsequent communication between them had to be by letter. Gerald followed the movements of his new friend with great interest, from Plymouth to Cornwall to Pangbourne to Saffron Walden to Cambridge to Bury St Edmunds and thence to Hull for the voyage to the Hook of Holland.

Fritz was enormously relieved to be going home to his family at last. He had not seen them since he was 18 years of age, and he was now nearly 22. However, despite his excitement, he was apprehensive about entering the Russian Zone of Germany. He had even heard rumours that the train would not stop in Germany but would take the men right through to Soviet Russia! This fear was not alleviated by the experiences in the trains themselves which "were in a most wretched state, many windows having been nailed up with wooden boards as substitute for the shattered glass panes, and they were bitterly cold." However, late on the evening of 27 November 1947, Fritz stood at the front door of the block of flats to which his parents had moved. He was back in Freital at last.

Back Home in Germany

Fritz's main memory of that time was the enormous amount of hope and the feeling of drawing close together. The worst of the food rationing was past, though there were of course still shortages. Everyone was absolutely clear that there must be no more war. It may not come as a surprise to hear that, with his love of languages and literature, Fritz decided to become a teacher. Some of the teachers from pre-war Germany had been dismissed by the Russian regime and replaced at this time by novice teachers who were rushed through a short period of training. A young lady teacher living next door offered Fritz advice about entering the profession, and when he was embarked on his career she gave him her support. Her name was Ilse, and she had in fact been one of Fritz's childhood playmates. Less than three years later he and Ilse were married. After further teacher training he was appointed in 1952 as a teacher of German and English at Freital Grammar School.

By this time five years had gone by since Fritz returned home. Most former prisoners of war, once they were immersed in their careers and married, naturally wished to put their past lives behind them and forget their wartime experiences. For Fritz it was different. He had made a close friend in England whom he was not inclined to forget. Nor did Gerald wish to forget him, as is evidenced by a photograph he had sent to Fritz at the camp in Basildon in July 1947. It showed Gerald, his mother and the dog, and on the back he had written, "To my dear friend Fritz. Hoping he will always remember me, as I will him. Gerald."

The postal friendship

As Fritz had no telephone, the only method of communication was by letter. Long letters with photographs and cuttings were exchanged, even on politically sensitive subjects such as unilateral disarmament, a nuclear free Europe and the destruction of Dresden. Despite postal censorship and restrictions on what one could send into the newly-formed "German

To my dear best friend Fritz. Hoping he will always remember me, as I will him.

Gerald.

Eileen, Bruno and
Gerald, on Gerald's
15th birthday, June
1947. Photograph
with message to
Fritz on reverse

Democratic Republic", most of the material arrived, and Fritz did not get into trouble for it. In the early 1950s, when Gerald was doing his National Service in the north of Germany, working on top secret ciphers, his letters to the East still reached Fritz. Only one item was confiscated at the border, because it was not on the GDR list of permitted printed material, a harmless geographical gazette addressed to Fritz's father.

Many of the picture postcards, folders, prospectuses and newspaper cuttings (which Fritz refers to as "counter-revolutionary paperclips"), proved exceedingly useful in his English classes. Little did Gerald guess, when he sent Fritz his school photograph showing his teacher, Mr Le Min, seated in the middle of the class wearing his formal academic gown, that the picture would be shown to all Fritz's new English classes. They looked at the teacher's attire with curiosity. Election communications from England were used also in class, and in fact everything of interest from England became a valuable visual aid for the teaching of English in an area where no other teacher would be likely to have access to such material. Sometimes Fritz and Gerald differed in their opinions on political and social matters, but they always appreciated each other's point of view. On one occasion Gerald's full description of the Cotswolds in a letter, accompanied by photographs, proved to be just what was needed to expand on a chapter in a textbook featuring the area. Gerald's enthusiasm for sending information was sometimes overwhelming. When Fritz asked if he could send him a picture of Charles Dickens suitable for a literature lesson, Fritz received an invitation from London to become a member of the Dickens Fellowship! Unfortunately he could not acquire convertible currency for the membership fee.

It was their mutual appreciation of classical music which perhaps played the largest part in the communications between the two men. One of the first records to arrive in Freital was Edward Elgar's *Enigma Variations*. Then came Ralph Vaughan Williams' *The Lark Ascending* followed by works of Gustav Holst, Benjamin Britten, William Walton, Michael Tippet, Herbert Parry, Peter Warlock, Gerald Finzi and Sir Arthur Bliss among others. There were hymns recorded in the cathedrals of Gloucester, Hereford and Worcester, and in King's College, Cambridge. There was music from the annual Three Choirs Festival and the Literature Festival of Cheltenham (where Gerald and his wife now lived in the suburb of Charlton Kings), and, of more personal interest, music from the Charlton Kings Choral Society in which Gerald sang tenor. None of these was ever confiscated at the border. It is highly likely that no such substantial collection of English classical music ever existed anywhere else in the German Democratic Republic. After the reunification of Germany, Fritz obtained more up-to-date equipment, and then Gerald could send tapes and CDs.

Although Fritz applied for permission to travel to England it was never granted during the 40-year life of the GDR. Sadly, therefore, he had to decline the invitation to Gerald's marriage to Christine Weller in August 1959, and to make do with a piece of wedding cake. Nor was it easy during those years for British people to visit the GDR. Announcements of the births of Fritz's three children and Gerald's two sons were sent in both directions as well as news of other family events and celebrations. The wives and the children too became part of the friendship, and both families rejoiced for each other's successes and grieved for each other's misfortunes. Their lives were going by, however, without the two friends managing to meet again. Gerald had been in West Germany several times, not only while doing National Service, but also to visit other former prisoners they had met in Plymouth. He wanted to take his wife and young

Gerald Towell's school photograph of 1948 showing teacher's academic gown, used by Herr Defèr in English classes

*Newspaper cutting sent by Gerald Towell to Fritz Defèr in GDR where
pupils were keenly interested in all attempts to ban nuclear weapons*

sons by car to visit Fritz and his family, but the restrictions and checks
required by the East German authorities were off-putting. He did not want to
put his family at risk, for example, by finding he had driven off the prescribed
route. The first "daring" trip to the East did at last take place, but it was by
train and nearly 40 years after Fritz's repatriation.

Ultimate Reunions
In March 1986, on a bitterly cold night with snow falling, Gerald and
his 22-year-old son Mark caught a train leaving Frankfurt at midnight
for Warsaw. They could not sleep on the overnight journey for excitement. East German guards searched their carriage but did not search
them. It was still dark when they arrived at Dresden station, the only
two people to disembark. There was just one person waiting on the
platform: it had to be Fritz. He took them home to Freital to meet his
wife Ilse and all their family. Their three children, Cornelia, Johannes
and Alexander, were all married. Their two grandsons were Winfried
aged four and Konrad aged one and a half. Gerald was embarrassed to
have brought a doll for Winfried, thinking that was a girl's name. But
what a glorious meeting it was! Fritz describes it thus: "We seemed to
understand each other at a glance. Might we not call it an extraordinary
friendship that not only did hold over so long a time, but furthermore
was not disappointed, when it had to be verified in reality. We had a
wonderful time together, seeing Dresden and its lovely surroundings."
Gerald remembers what marvellous evenings they enjoyed, just like a
family get-together. He also remembers his amazement at how towns
seemed to be decaying, with buildings looking as though they had not
been painted since before the war. Mark noticed the shortage of foods
in the shops and felt sorry for the people. Gradually, however, they began

to appreciate other aspects of the East German society, the warmth of family life and care for the elderly, how simple things were a pleasure without any feelings of greed, and the absence of the artificiality which the consumer society of the West can produce.

Gerald visited again at Easter 1988 when Fritz took him in his little Trabant car to Leipzig. There they stood together at the grave of Johann Sebastian Bach in front of the altar in the Thomas Church. From the central post office Gerald telephoned his parents, and Fritz spoke to Donald Towell, whose voice he had not heard for forty years, not knowing then that it would be his last conversation with him.

On the evening of the fall of the Berlin Wall, in November of the following year, Fritz and Ilse were visiting friends who owned a telephone. In that moment of euphoria Fritz rang Gerald to promise him it would not be long before they would see him in England. In the summer holidays of 1990 Fritz and Ilse spent a wonderful fortnight with Gerald and Christine at their home in Charlton Kings, Cheltenham. Unfortunately they had come a year too late to see Gerald's father again, but Mrs Eileen Towell, though suffering from dementia, immediately recognised "her Fritz". Gerald drove them to many different places and proved that, as a schoolboy, he really had read with care Fritz's early letters from camps in England, because he was able to say again and again, "That's where you were a POW."

A chance meeting at a concert between Gerald and Sir Arthur Bliss's widow some years earlier led eventually to Fritz's personal acquaintance with Lady Trudy Bliss. Apparently, in the early days of their marriage, Arthur and Trudy Bliss had had a particular interest in Austria and southern Germany. While enjoying a carefree holiday there in 1927, they were so enchanted by the views of the part of Germany known as "Saxon Switzerland" from the Vienna to Dresden train window that they alighted there unexpectedly. Through Gerald, Fritz had sent Lady Bliss a booklet on Saxon Switzerland in 1982. In return she had sent him a book of *Selected Writings On Music* by her late husband, Master of the Queen's Music, in which Fritz had been intrigued to read of the author's great appreciation of Johann Wolfgang von Goethe. Now he was in England, Fritz was able to take up Lady Bliss's invitation to visit her in her home in London, as he did in subsequent years also. Other visits with musical connections included in his itinerary were the birthplaces of Gustav Holst in Cheltenham, Edward Elgar near Worcester and Ralph Vaughan Williams near Cirencester.

The year 1990 proved to be the start of many visits to Britain for Fritz and Ilse, with return visits of Gerald and Christine to Germany. The four of them got on so well together that Fritz calls them "so good a team as if we were made for each other". Although Fritz had not been able

Christine and Gerald Towell at back, with Ilse
and Fritz Defèr, visiting Thuringia in 1997

to attend Gerald and Christine's wedding, all four were together for their 35th wedding anniversary in 1994, celebrating it on the Isle of Skye. The English couple still have the posy of wild flowers picked by Ilse as an anniversary surprise. "In some ways," says Fritz, "we feel like one kin," a surprising statement for a former prisoner of war to make about a former schoolboy from the country he had fought.

In the year 2000 it was Fritz and Ilse's turn to visit England. They came in the month of May as Fritz wanted to show Ilse the wonders of an English spring as he remembered them from former times. In particular the beauty of a bluebell wood was something Ilse had never experienced before, and the hedgerows were glorious with a wide array of wild flowers. Despite these shared interests, there are still some comical misunderstandings. The potpourri sent by Gerald to Fritz's daughter at Christmas that year was mistaken for English tea, and the family were made to drink an infusion of it! At the same Christmas the present of Stilton cheese reeked so much in Fritz and Ilse's flat that it had to be put out on the balcony.

Let Fritz's own words conclude the story, a story of a personal friendship which stood the test of decades of separation and still grows in strength as the years go by.

> Gerald and I are still old-fashioned enough to write long letters, send photos and pictures from our trips and what else we regard as worth to be known by the other one. As a matter of fact, since I have been initiated into the affluent western civilisation, I also own a telephone. But we only use it between ourselves to congratulate on a personal event or give an urgent message – and I am afraid to confess, as to Gerald and myself, to pull each other's legs. So let me end . . . with a limerick, which I dedicate to my English friends:
> There's a middle-aged couple at Charlton Kings,
> Who always think, when the telephone rings:
> Dear me! Is that Fritz,
> Still out of his wits –
> Or someone else, telling sensible things?

29. A Desire for Peace

At the end of the war, Henry Francies was a married man with two children, living northeast of London at Loughton in Essex. Ten years earlier he had hoped there would not be a war, and along with thousands of like-minded people had joined the Peace Pledge Union (PPU) with its pledge, "I renounce war and will never support or sanction another." Since then the war had come and gone, but the local Group of the PPU still met regularly under Henry's businesslike and punctilious leadership.

In 1946 the Group heard of the desperate shortage of food in Germany from Miss Elizabeth Fox Howard, a well-known Quaker living locally, who had visited the German Quaker headquarters at the spa town of Bad Pyrmont, near Hamelin. Henry Francies and his PPU Group responded by setting up a Famine Relief committee and sending food parcels to Germany and Austria, a task they continued for ten years. That same

Fritz Kübler aged 22, in his POW uniform at Lippetts Hill Camp in 1947

year they learnt that German prisoners of war in Britain were allowed to accept invitations to visit private houses. Not far away was a large camp of German prisoners, on the edge of Epping Forest at Lippitts Hill. Naturally keen to spread peace and reconciliation to former enemies who were on their doorstep, Henry and his Group led a local appeal for people willing to invite a prisoner into their home for Christmas Day.

On Christmas morning, Henry Francies, Peter Heathfield (mentioned elsewhere in this book) and Robert Long walked through the forest to collect some prisoners from the camp. Two men were allocated at random to Henry and his wife Nancy. They were Fritz Kübler, aged 22 with striking red hair, and an older family man, Karl Oëttinger, who came from Kiel in the northern limb of Germany not far from the Danish border.

Henry and Nancy's daughter Greta was eight years old and her sister Joan thirteen.

The visit of the prisoners made a big impression on Greta and seeing the men arrive at the front door in their camp uniforms is still vivid in her memory over fifty years later. She recalls that, in spite of an almost total lack of common language, they all had a very good time together as they enjoyed a traditional Christmas lunch. There was also a party in the local church hall, attended by many of the prisoners from the camp. Greta remembers the huge and beautifully decorated Christmas tree under which, after a good supper, the men sang carols in wonderful harmony. In particular she recalls that "the rendering of 'Silent Night' in German was sung with such feeling that it moved a number of people to tears".

Fritz and Karl must have been delighted to meet this very welcoming family. They started to visit them regularly, and sometimes took other prisoners. One was Jacob, a master baker, who saved up all the necessary ingredients and made a plate of beautifully crafted cakes in the shape of swans. Greta has never seen its like, before or since. Some prisoners were skilled at carving with pen-knives. They gave a wooden eagle and a life-size cuckoo to their newfound friends, each wing feather of the cuckoo carved from a separate piece of wood and carefully threaded together with wool. Some prisoners unpicked sacks to convert them cleverly into slippers.

When Karl Oëttinger was repatriated to his home-town of Kiel he found that his large family had been existing on a very poor diet, due to the shortage of food in the aftermath of the war. His oldest daughter, Rosemary, aged 20, had lost almost all her hair and a great deal of weight. An unusual arrangement was then made: she went to stay in Essex with the Francies family. Although there was rationing in Britain also, food was more nutritious and a considerable improvement on that available in Germany. The family received no extra coupons for rations to help feed their guest, but with a diet of plenty of fresh vegetables from Henry's allotment Rosemary's health and well-being greatly improved.

Fritz Kübler decided to stay in Essex after his release, working in local greenhouses growing tomatoes and flowers. He felt he was treated very fairly by his employer, Mr Harker, as he was given the same bonus at Christmas as were his English workmates. Fortunately, Fritz was living near enough to Loughton to continue visiting the Francies family. Greta remembers looking forward

Nancy, Joan, Henry and Greta Francies in their garden in 1948

to these events because they were always such fun with much laughter, and on Sundays Fritz would often bring a block of Neapolitan ice cream, a great treat. He called her his "little sister", and it was a nice feeling for Greta to have an "older brother" for the first time.

While working in Britain, Fritz attended language classes and learnt to speak English very quickly, perhaps as an aid to courting local girls! At one stage he moved to work in Scotland but became "homesick" for Essex. So, after visiting Germany for Christmas 1948, he returned to work in Essex for a further five years.

In 1950, Fritz Kübler and Henry and Nancy Francies made an unusual trip. Together the German man and the British couple paid a visit to Fritz's home village of Oberheinriet near Heilbronn, not far from Stuttgart, and were very well received. The villagers, many of whom had suffered greatly during the last period of the war, gave them a generous and kindly reception, and the village choir came out specially to sing to them. This and other similar experiences further convinced Henry of the value of a sympathetic approach to former "enemies" and the still vitally urgent need for compassion and understanding between nations.

During Fritz's time in England, Henry introduced him to what was to become a lifelong interest, football. They went together to White Hart Lane to watch Tottenham Hotspurs and to Wembley for the Cup Final. Fritz became a keen "Spurs" supporter. Many years later, after Fritz had returned to Germany and married Helga, a young woman from his own home-town, he trained as a football referee. He helped to establish a modern pavilion for his local football club. Remembering that it was in England he had learned to love the game, he became involved in the exchange of youth teams between Heilbronn and Cheshire. He acted as referee and interpreter for many years during these two-way visits.

Greta and her husband David now have three grown-up children, Ralph, Guy and Pippa. Fritz and Helga have a son, also called Ralph. The two families remain in close contact and have visited each other many times. Greta and David have made several recent trips to see Fritz and Helga in their home in the village of Oberheinriet and have welcomed them to their home in Oxford (see colour photographs). There is a regular exchange of letters, birthday and Christmas cards, and frequent telephone calls, especially when English and German football teams are playing each other. The friendships have deepened over the years, and during their latest visit Fritz's welcome for his "little sister" was as warm as ever. When Fritz had a four-month stay in hospital after a bad accident, Greta spoke to him by telephone every week to help cheer him up.

It all started with a desire for peace and reconciliation, and an offer of Christmas hospitality to strangers, but the friendships begun long ago still flourish into the new millennium and the next generation.

30. Friends Made, Lost and Found

Six Thousand Prisoners

Kurt Geibel was an 18-year-old paratrooper in the German Luftwaffe when he was captured by Canadians during the Battle for Holland in October 1944. As POW Number B 52387, he was first held at an assembly camp in Belgium and then shipped from Ostend, arriving in England in December. He remembers glimpsing Christmas trees through the windows of the English houses he was passing. The first British camp he was taken to was in Colchester where the accommodation was in tents. Here Kurt saw aircraft coming from many directions, meeting overhead and setting off for Germany in large formations of more than 100 planes. The thought that these bombers were destined for his own country led to much anxiety, as he had received no news from home and wondered about the safety of his parents and his brother, a pilot who was five years his senior. Because there had been rumours of Luftwaffe prisoners trying to escape to nearby airfields, Kurt was moved farther north to Mellands Camp, Gorton near Manchester. It was during his stay there that he was relieved to hear that the war in Europe was over and shortly afterwards he was moved to Glen Mill Camp in Oldham.

Glen Mill had been a working cotton mill from 1903 until 1938, situated

POW Kurt Geibel

in Wellyhole Street in the Lees area of Oldham. It was used as a POW camp from the beginning of the war, one of the first two POW camps to be opened. The four-floor building was of huge dimensions, each floor measuring about 100 yards by 80 yards (72,000 square feet). By the time Kurt arrived at Glen Mill Camp in mid 1945, over 6,000 prisoners were housed there, making it one of the largest prison camps in the country. On each of the first three floors of the mill, 2,000 prisoners had their quarters, sleeping in bunks three tiers high and only inches apart. The top floor was used as the hospital, and officers had to live in tents. The site was bordered by a road, a railway line and two reservoirs, with a cemetery nearby. One prisoner remarked, "All we could see was the graveyard. Funerals were the only excitement we had." Later the compound was enlarged to include an exercise yard and a football pitch (see colour photographs).

Picture sewn to inside of letter-form.
Kurt Geibel on right

Hope was aroused in the camp when the Red Cross supplied the prisoners with pre-paid search cards, a double postcard with room for the camp address and a short message. The other half of the card was returned if contact was made with relatives. In Kurt's case he heard that his parents were well, and his brother was in a military hospital, wounded when his plane had caught fire. It was a great relief when one or two letters could be sent home on the tuck-in letter-forms supplied. On one occasion Kurt sewed a photograph inside a letter-form: it arrived home safely. Prison life could be very boring, especially in the early days when no one was allowed to leave the camp. At this time an artists' corner was formed where any prisoner could demonstrate his artistic ability. Much of Kurt's time was spent in drawing and painting for which he had a wonderful talent. Drawings he made from small photographs of the children of fellow prisoners were exchanged for food, cigarettes and other valued items. Later, when the camp orchestra gave concerts, Kurt was responsible for designing and painting the scenery. He was to use his artistic talents as an etcher for the newspaper industry when he eventually returned home.

Kurt Geibel's drawings of children from the photographs of fellow prisoners

When prisoners were let out of the camp on supervised work parties, Kurt was part of a group helping with the building of 132 prefabricated houses in the Crete Street area of Oldham. The work involved laying sewers, making foundations for the "pre-fabs" which were later delivered in four parts, and preparing roads. It was hard work, but at least it brought relief from the cramped conditions and boredom of camp life. As Kurt was still a teenager, he was given the position of tea-boy, making the tea in a large bucket, distributing food and generally making himself useful.

Fraternisation with local people was not yet allowed, but Kurt managed to talk to some people passing along the street, though it had to be in a somewhat secretive manner. Some passers-by left biscuits and cakes behind the low walls of the small front gardens. The packages were not visible, but the prisoners knew they were there. On several occasions a policeman saw a conversation going on or food being passed over but turned the other way, much to Kurt's surprise.

A Young Man Makes Friends

A brick air-raid shelter was near the building site where Kurt was work-ing, which the prisoners began to use for tea breaks. Diagonally opposite the shelter lived Mrs Mary Walsh and her granddaughter Patricia, nearly five years of age. One day Patricia had a small accident with her scooter which broke in two parts. After Kurt used some screws to repair the scooter, a friendship with Patricia and her grandmother began. Patricia started bringing Kurt some lunch in a box, described by Kurt as "a wonderful lunch box which my own mother would have difficulty in surpassing". Despite rationing, Kurt was frequently given such food, enabling him to pass his own camp rations to his comrades. When Mrs Walsh told Kurt that she wished to be a mother to him during his stay in England, he felt that things were brightening up for him. Sometimes the courage of these newfound friends overwhelmed him: if people in Germany had shown such kindness to "the enemy" they would have been punished for it.

Kurt learnt much of his English from the children. He says,

They never grew tired of explaining how a new word had to be pronounced and the syllables stressed. They helped a great deal in improving my sparse knowledge of the English language.

Kurt made them toys, and slippers out of potato sacks. He enjoyed writing short letters to express his thanks for the kindnesses he received. He recalls,

This situation was very satisfying for me, since this act of letter writing was a help for me to learn English . . . . I loved making contacts and friends. I did learn a lot, and therefore it was a useful time for me too.

Kurt was fortunate to meet Mrs Mabel Blagbrough who showed an interest in prisoners at Glen Mill and did what she could to help them, but took particular notice of Kurt perhaps because of his young age. He saw her nearly every day and was able to have a chat and even exchange

short letters. On one occasion she prevented him from receiving 28 days'
detention when an English guard had
thought he was becoming too friendly
with English people during a football
match. She also wrote many times to
Kurt's parents in Germany and attempted to get him released early. Kurt may
not have realised at the time that she
was in touch with other people trying
to help prisoners, through such organisations as "Save Europe Now" and
"Prisoners of War Assistance (or Aid)
Society", but he was aware of her tireless work to help prisoners at the camp,
where she was known as "The Angel
of Glen Mill". He comments now,

Mabel Blagbrough, the
"Angel of Glen Mill"

> At such a young age I had never had
any contact with such an open, democratic way of life. And so,
despite the negative aspects of being a prisoner of war, I think that
my time in Britain . . . was good training for my later life in Germany.

These "beautiful friendships", as Kurt called them, were to come to
an abrupt halt after 18 months, in the autumn of 1946, when he was
suddenly moved to other camps, first in Surrey and then in Kent. But,
as soon as Mrs Walsh discovered Kurt's whereabouts she started to
send him letters, expressing her great concern to know how he was,
whether he had made new friends, and whether he could receive parcels.
If so, what would he like for his birthday? Sometimes she signed herself,
"Your English Mother". She was keen to give him news of Oldham: the
prefabs in Crete Street were completed, and people were living in them;
his prisoner friends had been moved to other camps and in a few cases
had been moved back again to Glen Mill, to the great joy of Mrs Walsh
and her friends. She also conveyed the sad news that her husband Joseph
had died suddenly at the age of 60. Patricia also wrote many letters in
neat capital letters in pencil.

Soon after Kurt left Oldham, fraternisation with British people was
officially permitted. As he was a cheerful man, he made many friends
with British people near the other camps to which he was moved. Via a
vicar who visited one of the camps, Kurt was sent paints by the artist
Richard Eurich, whose mother then corresponded with Kurt and with
his parents. He was not forgotten by the people of Oldham. On his
twenty-first birthday a postcard arrived at the camp in Beckenham, Kent,
from Mrs Mabel Blagbrough, and letters and a parcel from Mrs Walsh

Mrs Rennie, Patricia Rennie and Mrs Mary Walsh, Patricia's grandmother

and Patricia. For several months Mrs Walsh had been planning to send a present Kurt really wanted, a pair of shoes. The receipt was enclosed in case he needed to change them for a different size at another branch of Timpson's shoe shops. Thus he discovered the price, 32 shillings, a lot of money. The ration coupons had been supplied by another person in Oldham, Margaret Simms. Mrs Walsh also corresponded with Kurt's parents in Germany, getting their letters to her translated by the priest at St Patrick's Church. By this time, British people were allowed to send food parcels to Germany, so Mrs Walsh sent one to Mr and Mrs Geibel, which arrived by chance on Christmas Eve.

Kurt was moved to several other camps including one in Scotland and still Mrs Walsh kept in touch. After his move to Scotland she wrote, "Now to a little motherly advice. You will find living in the north not like the south of England. The climates are two extremes. So watch your health for catching the cold. Remember this please." In total, Kurt saw the insides of 12 camps before he heard he was to be sent home after almost four years as a prisoner. He had managed to earn some money from doing jobs for English families. He exchanged some of it for clothes coupons and purchased a suit before he was repatriated, otherwise he would have had to arrive home in his POW uniform. Due to the dire shortages of all kinds of goods in Germany, that suit was much admired in Kurt's home-town, especially by the young women, and the shoes from Mrs Walsh remained his best pair for a long time.

The strength of the friendships made in Oldham was such that on Kurt's repatriation to Frankfurt-am-Main in April 1948, both parties were keen to keep in touch. For some time letters were exchanged. Kurt's sister-in-law who had a young daughter, Marianne, wrote to Patricia, but Marianne was four years younger than Patricia and too young to become a pen-friend. Kurt was married in 1950 and was then busy trying to get on in his profession as a rotogravure-etcher in a newspaper printing factory, working in the basement of a partially destroyed building surrounded by rubble. This period of reconstruction in Germany left hardly any time for leisure activities, so contact was lost with his English friends, something Kurt regretted over the years.

A Journey of Hope

The story skips forward forty years to June 1988, when Herr Kurt Geibel, by now nearing the end of his successful career in the newspaper industry, made an unusual decision. He found his old shoe box, in which he had kept the yellowing letters and old photographs from his POW days, and determined to make a journey from his home in Dietzenbach, near Frankfurt-am-Main, to Oldham in the north of England in the slight hope of renewing old friendships. His wife Maria did not wish to accompany him, feeling that he should leave the past behind. Travelling on his own by car and ferry via Rotterdam and Hull, he reached Oldham and went to the area where he had worked 40 years before. He knew no one, and the house where Mrs Walsh and Patricia had lived had long since been demolished.

With a handful of fading photographs, Kurt approached a man sitting in front of a house in a nearby street. The man was kind enough to make a few telephone calls on Kurt's behalf, and within hours he had a bed for the night in the home of a lady who remembered him. She was Mrs Marian Wood, who as the shy teenager Marian Riley, used to hurry past the building site where Kurt and his fellow prisoners worked, and so gained the nickname of "Spitfire" because of her speedy walk. Kurt learned that Mrs Walsh had died 20 years before, Patricia had married and moved away, and Glen Mill had been demolished. But his visit was not to be in vain, for the following day he had an invitation to meet the Mayor of Oldham, Councillor Harry Slack. This meeting led to an article and photographs in the *Oldham Evening Chronicle* headed "I Will Never Forget", which was to produce further results in due course.

After staying three days in Oldham, visiting the areas of the town he remembered and the site of Glen Mill where a different factory now stood, Herr Geibel continued his journey north to Scotland. He reached Loch Ness and Inverness where he had spent time in a small camp, a satellite of the camp at Brahan Castle in Dingwall, and found the remains of his old camp. As a prisoner he had seen road signs to Fort Augustus and Fort William, and he remembered thinking how much he would like to visit them. Now, 40 years later, he was able to do so. In recalling this trip, he adds, "I also reached the summit of Ben Nevis, Britain's highest mountain, on 19 June 1988. I have the certification, together with a stone from the summit, hanging framed in my room."

*Patricia's children, Vanessa and Timothy, looking
at old documents, with Kurt Geibel in 1996*

The feature in the *Oldham Evening Chronicle* included an old photograph of Patricia as a child. This found its way to Patricia, who was by then Mrs Nicholls, a middle-aged language teacher, living in Blackpool, with three grown-up children. She wrote to Kurt and arranged to meet him on his next visit to Oldham, when a happy reunion took place. She promised to visit Germany the following year, but first her son was to get married, and she was to go into hospital. Very sadly this next meeting never happened as Patricia died in August 1990 just before her 50th birthday. With the untimely death of Mrs Patricia Nicholls perhaps the most important part of this 40-year-old story came to a sad end.

There was another result of the newspaper article, however, which was to lead to a new wave of friendships between Herr Geibel and the people of Oldham. Saddleworth Male Voice Choir, founded in 1955 and winner of many music festivals, had hosted a choir from Germany the previous October, and by coincidence this German choir, "Sängervereinigung Oberrodenbach ", was from a small town near where Kurt now lived. It too was a male voice choir, founded in 1878 and winner of choir festival prizes, including second place in the Montreux International Choir Festival. Having seen the article about Herr Geibel in the newspaper, the Saddleworth choir wrote to the German choir and asked if it could be arranged for them to meet Kurt during their forthcoming visit to Germany.

Thus began some new friendships with the people of Oldham, members of the choir, and in particular with Mr and Mrs Paul Johnson. As Kurt's exploratory trip turned out so well, his wife Maria is now always with Kurt on his regular visits to England. Kurt and Maria Geibel and Paul and Kathleen Johnson have become great friends. During one visit of the Saddleworth Choir to Germany, Kurt discovered that a member of the choir had the surname Blagbrough. Eddie Blagbrough was a great grandson of Mabel Blagbrough, and so, on this visit to Germany, Eddie – to his surprise – learnt new things about the brave and principled lady, his great grandmother, the Angel of Glen Mill.

A Surprise Gift

Even this is not quite the end of the story. Kurt believed strongly that the kindness he had been shown as a prisoner of war in Oldham should be known by future generations. He had always had a feeling that he must somehow thank the British people once more for this kindness and give something back to the town of Oldham. He therefore put together into a large ring binder all the papers, letters and photographs which he had now kept safe for 50 years, many of great sentimental value to him, and he briefly wrote down the story of his experiences as a POW in England. He had determined to give this collection of letters, pictures and stories to the people of Oldham. So, in October 1997, at 71 years of age, Herr Geibel again visited Oldham, this time to present his book to the Mayor and Mayoress, Councillor Peter Dean and Mrs Susan Dean, as a "thank you" for all the warmth shown to him in the past. In his Foreword Kurt wrote,

These are the letters which were written by British mothers and families who went to great lengths to ensure that a then 18-year-old German prisoner of war endured his long period of capture without too many hardships. They were in part written at a time when any fraternisation with German prisoners in Britain was forbidden and a punishable offence . . . . Of course I also contravened the regulations at that time, but that was possible with a few tricks. Many people wanted to help and carefully disregarded the rules and regulations. I don't know another country in which this would have been possible at that time.

The book is now in Oldham Local Studies Library for the public to read at their leisure. A further copy is deposited at Eden Camp Modern History Theme Museum in Malton, North Yorkshire. Kurt's hope is that coming generations will "get an impression of those days" and will learn "how nice the people of Oldham were" to him and realise how much good can come out of something as terrible as war.

Herr Kurt Geibel presenting his book to the Mayor and Mayoress of Oldham, Councillor Peter Dean and Mrs Susan Dean, and Mrs Mary Wood, October 1997 (Oldham Evening Chronicle)

31. A Forty-Year-Old Letter

Mr Hugh Williams was managing a farm in West Haddon not far from Rugby in 1947, having served in the Commando Regiment during the war. Several German POWs came from a camp near Long Buckby to work on the farm. One of them, Peter Göbel, had been a farmer himself in Germany, and at the age of 34 was a few years older than Mr Williams. When Peter was invited to spend Christmas Day 1947 at the farm with Hugh and Marjorie and their two-year-old daughter Glenys, he gave the little girl a push-along wooden duck with wings which flapped as it moved: he had made it himself.

The following March, Peter's days as a POW were thankfully over, and he was sent back to Germany, arriving at his farm in Dahlem in Rheinland on 13 March 1948. There he found his wife, his sister, brother-in-law and two-year-old niece all in good health, contrary to his expectations, although the farm itself had suffered through the war and through absence of farm workers. To get it back into good working order, he had a big task ahead of him to make up for the time he had spent as a POW in England.

Just before Christmas 1948 he thought back with fond memories to the Christmas of the year before. He typed a letter in faltering English and sent it to Mr Williams, telling how he had arrived back home in the spring and had set to work improving the farm. The letter went on to say,

Christmas will come soon! I think often [of] the nice Christmas time in your lovely house. You [treated] me not as a prisoner of war, but more [as] a gentleman . . . . I couldn't forgotten the nice time with you . . . . I do thank [you] for all [the] presents before my depart[ure] . . . . I'm very obliged to wish lots of luck, merry Christmas, and New Year with health, prosperity all round the corner. From your sincerely, Peter Göbel.

For some reason this letter was never answered. Later in life Mr Williams admits that he "sat on it", but fortunately he did not destroy it.

Forty years later Glenys's husband, Keith Spittlehouse, visited Germany several times from his home in Devon. He had heard about the brief friendship with German prisoners after the end of the war, and he wondered whether it would be possible to trace his in-laws' long lost acquaintance, Peter Göbel. In 1988 Mr Williams found the 1948 letter, and a copy was forwarded via the German Embassy to the Mayor of Bitburg who, amazingly, was able to discover Herr Göbel. In true farming tradition he was still tilling the same land in Dahlem, ten kilometres from Bitburg.

Imagine Herr Göbel's surprise to receive a response to his letter of 40 years before, forwarded to him from the Mayor! He described it as "wonderful" that Mr Williams remembered him, though he himself had never forgotten those days and often talked about his time in England and the English family at the farm near Rugby. The accompanying message indicated that some of the family would be coming to the region and would like to meet Peter. By this time he was aged 75 and delighted at the prospect of seeing his English friends once more. He asked his daughter-in-law to write back in English to find out when the proposed visit would take place, enclosing a photograph of himself with his wife and their granddaughter, so that Mr Williams could "see how I look today".

Hugh and Marjorie Williams, their daughter Glenys and her husband Keith, went to Germany later that year and met up with Peter Göbel, his wife Elizabeth, their two sons Dieter and Johann, and Johann's wife and daughter. The English visitors were made to feel very welcome indeed and were led around the village of Dahlem, to meet relatives and friends. They spoke very little German but fortunately Peter's nephew, Werner, spoke good English, having worked on a US air-force base in the area. Peter had not needed to use English since 1948, but his recollection of the language improved during the day "with the flow of wine". The wonderful reunion for the older generation proved also to be an interesting meeting for the younger members of the two families.

After that, the German family travelled to England on several occasions to see Mr and Mrs Williams, who were living in Surrey. Unfortunately Peter himself did not come as he was in poor health at the time of the first visit and died in the mid-1990s. His widow, Elizabeth, her brother and his wife, her granddaughter and her nephew all made the trip to Surrey. Although Mr Williams died in 2001, correspondence continues between the families several times a year, and nowadays a letter no longer remains unanswered!

In Dahlem, Germany in 1988. Top row: Elizabeth Göbel and Dieter Göbel. Middle row: Hugh Williams, Johann's wife, Peter Göbel, Glenys and Keith Spittlehouse. Bottom row: Martine Göbel (Johann's daughter), Johann Göbel and Marjorie Williams

32. The Young Man with a Conscience

Essex boy Peter Heathfield had always had an interest in things German. His best friend at primary school in Ilford in the 1930s was a boy with a German mother and a father who had been in the British army of occupation in the Rhine after the First World War, meeting his future wife in Cologne. Peter often saw his school friend's German grandmother, heard the family talking German and looked at German children's books.

This was not Peter's only reason for being unwilling to fight against Germany when the Second World War came. He was a conscientious objector, believing that to take up arms against fellow human beings could never be right. He had links with organisations with similar beliefs such as the Fellowship of Reconciliation, the International Friendship League, the Methodist Peace Fellowship, the Society of Friends (Quakers) and the Peace Pledge Union.

After the war, in December 1946 when Peter was aged 23 and living in Loughton, Essex, the local Group of the Peace Pledge Union discussed the news that German prisoners could now be invited into private homes. As a result, Peter and his older friend Henry Francies (mentioned elsewhere in this book) agreed to contact Protestant clergy to ask if members of their congregations would offer Christmas Day hospitality to prisoners in the nearby POW camp at Lippitts Hill, Epping Forest. The Roman Catholics had already made such arrangements for prisoners who attended their church in Chingford.

Peter felt that the response was disappointing. In the first place, some clergy refused to get involved. Secondly, only eight families in the Loughton area were willing to invite a prisoner to their homes for Christmas Day, and Peter's own family was not among them. Peter's mother was prepared to do so, but his father said that if she wished to invite Germans into the house it would have to be when he was not there. Mr Heathfield had been a sergeant major in the First World War. In fact, so keen had he been to enter the army that he falsified his age. He experienced trench warfare, had been wounded and gassed, and held the common view that Germans were responsible for both wars and were a menace. He was very critical of his own brother who, as a conscientious objector in the First World War, had been imprisoned for his stance for two and a half years. Nor did he understand his son Peter's reasons for being unwilling to fight.

Although Peter was not able to entertain a prisoner in his own home on Christmas Day, he was invited to help his married friend Henry Francies in his home on Christmas Day, and there he met a prisoner named Fritz Kübler. He managed also to meet other prisoners by regularly turning up at the camp gate. On one such occasion the British Officer in Charge asked Peter to spare him a moment and took him into his office. He explained that he would like Peter's help as the prisoner who was giving English lessons to fellow prisoners was aware that his colloquial English was inadequate. Would Peter be prepared to invite this man, Karl Behringer, to his home and give him lessons in everyday English usage? Although there was no remuneration, Peter readily agreed, the only problem being that Karl had to be careful to visit Peter at times when it was known that his father would not be at home.

Karl Behringer
Karl enjoyed his visits to Peter's house and was anxious to show his appreciation. Being a very practical man of 26 years of age, he began to do all sorts of odd jobs around the house, tasks which Peter's father never seemed to have time to do. Mr Heathfield found out that these jobs were being done, so Peter and his mother had to explain what had

been happening, but to their utter surprise, Mr Heathfield expressed a wish to meet Karl. Faced with the ordinary individual German he overcame his prejudice and came to see that Germans were also human beings! Indeed he said to his wife, "They had no choice but to fight, they were conscripted and did what they thought was right." Eventually Mr Heathfield and Karl Behringer became very good friends. Karl also started to teach Peter to speak German.

During 1947 Karl received the good news that he was soon to be repatriated to his home-town of Kirchheim unter Teck, southeast of Stuttgart. Peter was keen to continue learning German so he asked if Karl knew a prisoner who might be prepared to carry on the lessons, and also perhaps receive English

Peter Heathfield and Karl Behringer at Woodford Green, Essex, in 1947

lessons from Peter. Thus "Christian" was introduced to the family. (Three years later Peter discovered that his real name was Christoph and that "Christian" was a nickname which he thought would be easier for English people to accept.)

Karl also asked whether the Heathfield family would befriend Heinz Riemann, another man from the camp, one who had received no invitations to visit English families and was somewhat depressed. This they gladly agreed to do and from then on Mr Heathfield made no objection to visits from prisoners and indeed was always friendly towards them. Heinz visited the family for a few months before being repatriated to the eastern zone of Germany.

Christoph Gaudlitz

It was "Christian" who was to become the greatest friend. Christoph Gaudlitz, who came from Dresden, had been part of the German occupation in Jersey for a few months before being taken prisoner in 1944 at the age of 20. He visited Peter and his parents regularly, being treated like another son. By this time, prisoners were allowed to use public transport, so Peter and Christoph often travelled the 20 miles to London to attend concerts and the theatre.

As a child up to the age of eleven and before moving to Dresden, Christoph had lived in the nearby Erzgebirge District of Saxony not far from the Czech frontier, an area famous for wood carvers whose speciality at Christmas was the "Christmas Pyra-

Christoph Gaudlitz in his POW uniform in 1947

mid" or Carousel. This wooden creation contains a delicately painted nativity scene, above which is fixed a metal plate, so cut and bent that heat from candles below drives the whole structure round and round. Christoph must have seen many of these intriguing novelties in his childhood, so he set himself the task of making one as a gift for Peter. Using plywood, stiff card and an old piece of metal he created the carousel with great skill and ingenuity. It was enjoyed every Christmas for about 20 years until it fell apart.

Friendships on the Building Site

As a conscientious objector in 1942, Peter had been directed by the National Service Office to undertake agricultural work. He had spent two years away from home as a farm labourer in Worcestershire, but, when this became too strenuous for him, he successfully applied to have his conditions changed, being permitted to do clerical work in the spheres of health or building operations. When at last the extreme shortage of building materials ended, he obtained a position only a mile from his parents' home in Loughton. It was in the buyer's office of a building firm which was under contract to the London County Council to build a large London "overspill" housing estate at Debden. In 1947 a gang of about 200 German POWs was brought to work at the building site, travelling by lorry from places such as Tottenham to the southwest and Fairlop to the southeast, some having a one-hour journey each way every day. Peter did not normally come into contact with these prisoners as his own work was confined to the office.

However, in an emergency during the very cold winter of 1947, Peter was told to go to the main gate of the building site to receive deliveries of building supplies. A group of prisoners was always available to unload lorries, and so it was now Peter with whom they liaised. He became acquainted with some of the men, who soon discovered his sympathy with their situation. He learnt that Hans Koreng from Saxony, had a double rupture and yet, back at the camp, was being made to lift and carry heavy bags of material and large planks of wood. Peter remembered speaking to him and noticing that he looked "poorly and frail", but later he became more ill. Through Peter's contacts with London Young Friends (Quakers), he learned that the Quaker "Committee for Refugees and Aliens" might be able to take action in cases of prisoners' difficulties. He gave them details of Hans Koreng, and in turn, they passed the information to the International Red Cross. The result seems to have been that, as soon as the authorities heard that enquiries were being made about any prisoner, the one concerned was repatriated without delay. Such cases of inappropriate treatment of prisoners in British camps were probably rare.

By this time Peter was no doubt getting a reputation among some of the Germans, as a young man with a conscience who cared about their situation and could be very helpful to them. He received a request regarding the sale of artifacts which the prisoners made out of discarded materials. They collected offcuts of wood to make ingenious toys and beautiful wooden boxes and other carved objects. Peter was astonished at their versatility. A delivery of such items would be made to Peter regularly, and he had some success in persuading friends to purchase them. He still possesses some little wooden boxes and one carved book end of what was originally a pair.

The next request was that Peter should use the money obtained from these sales, to buy tinned food. Then he was asked to send the tins in small parcels to the prisoners' homes in Germany. Food was also donated by well-wishers, quite a sacrifice in those days of rationing. In such ways as these Peter got to know many prisoners through his workplace, but most of them were in camps too far away to be invited home. One exception was Artur Gernt who was at a camp about five miles away, near enough to visit Peter's home, which he was pleased to do.

Books and Papers

Many camps produced a regular camp newspaper for internal circulation. Peter was given some of these by his prisoner friends, to assist him in improving his understanding of the German language. He also acquired some paperback editions of German classical literature, by such authors as Johann Wolfgang von Goethe and Heinrich von Kleist, which had been printed in German in large quantities by the World's Alliance of YMCAs as suitable reading material for prisoners of war, to help them to make the most of their spare time (see colour photographs).

In 1948 Peter went to stay with a friend, Kenneth Bond, who lived near Accrington in Lancashire, having first met him during his farm labouring days as a conscientious objector when they were boarded together at a farmhouse in a village near Evesham in Worcestershire. During Peter's visit to Lancashire, the two of them travelled across the Pennines by bus to Yorkshire to visit places of interest such as Skipton, Bolton Abbey, Fountains Abbey, Harrogate and, as "fans" of the Brontë sisters, Haworth. While having coffee one morning in a café in Skipton, they were surprised to see a number of German POWs. Peter got talking to them, using such German phrases as he knew and was given a copy of the Skipton camp newspaper. Then a prisoner who had been in a camp in Ripon, promised to send Peter a copy of that camp's newspaper too. Most of Peter's collection of camp newspapers has by now disintegrated, being printed on cheap, grey, wartime paper, but the copy of *Die Pforte* (The Door) from Ripon still remains in a readable condition over half a century later (see colour photographs).

Another prisoner, Christoph Juneman, who, like many, had first been a prisoner in USA, was a devout

An original list of a few of the many books printed in German for prisoners by the YMCA in the series known as "Zaunkönig Bücher"

Zaunkönig, literally "king of the fence", is the German word for "wren". The symbol printed on the books shows a wren perched on a barbed wire fence and wearing a crown!

Roman Catholic who went regularly to church in Chingford where he was a server at Mass. He had been issued with two hymn books, one in USA and the other in England. He discovered that Peter was a great lover of church music with a particular interest in hymns, so when he left England, he gave him his two music hymn books. Subsequently Peter made a study of German and British hymnody, with special reference to the inclusion of German hymn tunes and German translated words in British hymn books.

Long-lasting Friendships
This short period in Peter's life, as a young man of 23 and 24, soon came to an end, but his interest in so many POWs gave rise to many continuing friendships. He spent much of his career in teaching, but at one time he was writing conscientiously to about 20 former prisoners who had returned to Germany. He recalls that "it became too much and dwindled to five". Over fifty years later, he still has regular correspondence with, and visits the families of, four former prisoners. Peter has great respect for these four men. He feels that, despite humble beginnings, they all showed tremendous courage and initiative in the way in which they struggled to rebuild their lives after their wartime experiences.

First there was Karl Behringer. He became a manager in a catering business. In 1950 Peter received a warm invitation from his family to visit their house in Kirchheim, southeast of Stuttgart. As a single man, Peter was able to visit Germany most years from then onwards and get to know the family well. He grew very fond of Karl's mother who was always very kind to him and lived to nearly 100. He also knew all three of Karl's brothers. The friendship with Karl lasted through his terminal illness, Peter visiting him only two weeks before his death in 1997 at the age of 76.

Second was Artur Gernt. When Artur was repatriated from the camp in

Artur Gernt at Fairlop Camp in 1947

Essex, he returned home to Brandenburg in the east of Germany near Berlin. His mother told him he would be wise to go to join his brother who had already moved west, so Artur settled in Wuppertal in Westphalia where he met his future wife. Peter has very often been to the Wuppertal area to visit Artur and his wife, their children and, later, their families too.

Third was Fritz Kübler, one of the original prisoners given hospitality in Loughton on Christmas Day 1946. Peter met him many times during his prisoner days at the home of his friend Henry Francies, and remained in touch with him later when Fritz stayed on in Britain to work, before eventually returning to Germany. Several times Peter visited his parents' house near Heilbronn, north of Stuttgart, and then a beautiful house Fritz and his wife built for themselves and their son outside the village.

The fourth former prisoner with whom Peter is still in contact is, of course, his close friend Christoph Gaudlitz. An early invitation came from Christoph's parents to visit them in Dresden, but Peter was unable to obtain a visa to enter East Germany. Christoph sent Peter many postcards of his beloved Dresden, showing the wonderful baroque architecture before its destruction in the bombing of 13 February 1945. In 1950, before the era of the Berlin Wall, when people could travel freely within that city's limits, Peter managed to meet the family in Berlin. Christoph and Peter stayed with Christoph's cousin in West Berlin. Christoph's parents stayed with relatives in East Berlin. They all met each day for meals either in the homes of their relatives or in the communist run restaurants known as H.O. ("Handels Organisation", meaning a trading unit). This was when Peter found out for the first time that "Christian" was not Christoph's actual name!

Peter at last obtained a visa to go to Dresden in 1985, and then he could see for himself "how dismal and depressing" life in the German Democratic Republic had become. Christoph had chosen to stay in the East rather than desert his elderly parents, but he and his wife and daughter had not fared well there, due to their preference for having links with the Lutheran Church rather than assiduously attending state ceremonies. They refused to go along with the political activities expected of workers and suffered poor health due to the stress this entailed. After the reunification of Germany, Christoph and his wife were glad to move west and now live near Cologne where Peter still corresponds with them.

Peter's ongoing friendships with so many former prisoners was strengthened during a five-year period which he himself spent living in Germany. Thanks to the help with the German language given him by Karl and Christoph, he felt able to study in Stuttgart in 1958. He spent a year at the international seminary of "The Christian Community", a religious movement which had been established earlier in the century with the help of the Austrian philosopher and educationalist, Rudolf Steiner. Then he moved to a Steiner School 25 miles east of Stuttgart, situated in an area of great natural beauty, where he worked in one of the hostels for boarders, taught English and helped with the music. He became a fluent German speaker during this period, and of course visited many former prisoners, as well as people who had suffered during the Nazi era. Peter's mother joined him in Germany for a time and was able to visit Karl Behringer and his wife and family, who "made a great fuss of her".

A few years ago Peter threw away many papers: he was simply over-whelmed by the amount that he had collected over the years. "Some things had to go," he says. Now, well into his 70s, as he looks at what memorabilia he still has from those times, he can reflect with some pride on the help he was able to offer to so many of the pris-oners of war. His uppermost feel-ing, however, is gratitude for the generous hospi-tality he has received in Ger-many over the last 50 years, for which he feels greatly indebted to his many Ger-man friends.

Peter Heathfield in the year 2000 with wooden artifacts (two boxes and one of a pair of book ends) made by Christoph Gaudlitz, and some of the booklets given to him by other prisoners. The larger box has a lid, and a raised lip in the lower half so that it closes perfectly. The smaller box has a separate grooved lid

33. The Broken Link

In January 1947 Mr and Mrs Conway lived in Park Road, Accrington in Lancashire. They heard that contact was now allowed between German prisoners of war and British people. Knowing there were prisoners in a camp in a nearby village, they decided to invite one for Sunday lunch. After all, they were all "somebody's sons". The prisoner who was dropped off from an army waggon in Park Road on that particular Sunday was Heinz Schallenbach, aged 22.

Mr and Mrs Conway's 15-year-old daughter, Noreen, was surprised to see that the prisoner had a patch on his back with the initials POW. She remembers how well they all got on together on that first Sunday. The result was that Heinz was invited to come again, and from then on he visited most Sundays. He walked the three miles each way between the camp and Accrington for five months whatever the weather, during the very bad winter of 1947. In May he was moved to a camp in Bury, but the friendship was so important that he managed to travel regularly the 15 miles north to the house in Accrington.

When Heinz returned to his home-town of Altena in northwest Germany in December that year, he was keen to keep in touch with the family. At the time, Noreen was preparing for her School Certificate examinations, and she told Heinz all about them in many letters. Eventually the correspondence petered out, and the link was broken: no one now remembers why. This could well have been the end of the story.

Heinz Schallenbach, centre, with fellow prisoners, Willi Stracke from Westphalia and Heiner Scherer from Frankfurt. Outside the huts at Stanhill Hostel, Oswaldtwistle, November 1946

About thirty years later, early in 1979, Herr Heinz Schallenbach was working in the publicity department of the Town Hall in Altena. The town was twinned with Peronne in France, and Peronne was twinned with Blackburn in Lancashire. Therefore the

Laying pavements and foundations for prefabricated houses near Wigan in May 1947. Heinz Schallenbach back row, second right

town of Altena decided to set up a link with Blackburn, so that all three towns could be connected. Knowing that Blackburn was only a few miles from Accrington, Heinz took the opportunity to go to Blackburn to help in the setting up of the scheme, very much hoping that, while there, he would be able to call to see Mr and Mrs Conway and Noreen. He had always felt grateful for their friendship and kindness during his prisoner-of-war days, and he wanted to be able to show his appreciation in some way. Blackburn Councillor, Mr Malcolm Smith, arranged for a Rolls Royce to take Herr Schallenbach to Park Road, Accrington, but much to Heinz's disappointment the Conway family was no longer there. Unknown to him, both Mr and Mrs Conway had died, the house had long since been sold, and Noreen was now Mrs Almond, living with her husband, Bob, and their three children, in the neighbouring town of Oswaldtwistle. Herr Schallenbach returned to Germany feeling upset at not managing to contact his former friends.

However, Councillor Smith promised to keep up the search. He found out that there was a Mrs Conway who was a school librarian, but this turned out to be no relation at all. Fortunately the librarian knew Noreen, as, not only had she taught at that same school in the past, but also the librarian's husband had lived next door to Noreen's father in their boyhood! She told Mr Smith of Noreen's whereabouts and even telephoned Noreen who then telephoned Councillor Smith, and was given the address

Taking a break from laying foundations for prefabs. Heinz Schallenbach second row, third from right

The first meal of the first visit to Oswaldtwistle after being reunited in 1979. Heinz and Erna Schallenbach with Bob, Carol and David Almond. Noreen Almond took the photo

of the Town Hall in Altena, and wrote a letter there addressed to Herr Heinz Schallenbach. Although her memories of Heinz after over 30 years were rather dim, she was very happy about the idea of re-establishing the link.

A speedy reply came, complete with photographs of Heinz, his wife Erna and their 20-year-old son, Michael, and an invitation to visit them in Altena. Noreen's husband was reluctant to take up this sudden offer of hospitality from a stranger, especially as he spoke no German. Instead, they decided to invite Heinz and Erna to visit *them* in Oswaldtwistle. The invitation was immediately accepted, and the visit took place at the Spring Bank Holiday that same year.

Erna did not speak English, but Heinz's English was very good. David Almond, Noreen and Bob's younger son, was learning German at school. Their daughter Carol, came home from Aston University, Birmingham, for the weekend to meet Herr and Frau Schallenbach. With no difficulty they all became good friends. The two couples went up to the Lake District where Noreen and Bob had a caravan. They left their German friends there to spend the rest of the week at the caravan while they returned home to go to work. Now, many years later, Noreen remembers how hard it was at the time to believe that Germans had ever been our enemies.

David was to take his O-level examinations the following year so he was invited to stay with Heinz and Erna in the summer to improve his German. He was treated extremely kindly, and he benefited tremendously from the visit, for not only did he pass the exam, but German became one of his university subjects. He kept in touch with Heinz and his family during his student days, visiting them on several occasions. When David and one of his student friends arrived with rucksacks in Altena, they were always made most welcome, accommodated,

Noreen Almond with Erna and Heinz Schallenbach in the Lake District, while staying in the caravan in April 1979

fed and had their laundry done before setting off again on their travels. In return, when Heinz and Erna's son Michael came to Britain on a touring holiday with a friend and paid a visit to Accrington, Noreen tried to repay Erna's kindness by doing all their washing and ironing prior to departure.

The friendship developed so naturally that Bob lost any hesitation about going to stay in Germany. In 1980 Noreen, Bob and David went to Altena and had a very happy holiday

Noreen Almond with Erna and Heinz Schallenbach enjoying a holiday together in Austria. Bob Almond was taking the photo

there being treated "like royalty" as Noreen's birthday happened to fall while they were in Germany. The birthday celebrations lasted all week, and Noreen was showered with roses. While staying in Altena, she was shown a pile of letters she had apparently written to Heinz in her youth, which he had carefully preserved. She was surprised to see them, hardly being able to recall writing them at all!

Another year they all met in Austria for a holiday together in Seefeld in Tirol. Later, when Noreen and Bob removed in 1989 from Accrington to Saundersfoot on the South Wales coast, their German friends visited them there, and David came to stay for the weekend to see them again.

In October 1998, Noreen and Bob again went to Germany, unsure for how long they would feel able to drive so far. While they were in Altena, David, now himself living and working in Germany, came one weekend, and so did Heinz and Erna's son Michael (married with two children), and so the two sons had the opportunity to meet again after a gap of time. David then took his parents and Heinz and Erna the 80 miles to the town where he was living, Holzminden, where he had arranged accommodation for them in a hotel so he could show them the area. Amid the scent of pine woods and wonderful scenery, they had a most enjoyable holiday.

Thus the link between Heinz and Noreen, which started with a simple meal in 1947, was re-established after thirty years due to a deep feeling of gratitude. It grew to encompass both families, resulting in an enduring friendship. Every New Year's Day Heinz and Erna telephone their British friends, intent on ensuring that the precious link is never again broken.

34. A Bridge of Friendship

In December 1946, Arthur Durrant of Dagenham was thrilled to hear it announced on the wireless that people could invite German prisoners of war into their homes for Christmas Day. He had been a conscientious objector during the war, as a result of having formed close links with some members of the German YMCA in Berlin, and also due to his Christian faith. He felt he could not take up arms against his friends.

At the end of the war, Arthur had the strong feeling that he must somehow build a bridge of friendship between English and German people across the ruins. In fact, although he lived in Dagenham in East London his first step towards this aim, as it happened, was to make a link with a German prisoner in Lancashire. This occurred when he was staying with friends near Clitheroe in July 1946. He had decided to have an afternoon on his own on the moor overlooking the village of Newton on the Lancashire/Yorkshire border. When it started to rain he ran for shelter to a large tree. Someone else did the same, and Arthur found himself face to face with a 19-year-old German prisoner, Max Midasch, who was working on a local farm. The relationship which developed from this chance encounter was the first stage in Arthur's bridge of friendship.

Christmas 1946 provided Arthur with the second step in achieving his goal. When he heard the wireless announcement he discussed possibilities with friends at Kingsley Hall Christian Community Centre in Dagenham where he was a helper in the youth club. Although Dagenham had been heavily bombed during the war, it was agreed that this opportunity should not be lost and some action should be taken. Arthur and a friend who could speak German went to the POW camp at Harold Wood, Essex on Christmas Day. Arthur explained that "Six prisoners in their rough clothes were introduced, and the last one, a fair-haired young fellow, looked straight at me. We winked at each other as I signed papers which guaranteed that I would keep them sober and bring them back in good order by 9 pm. We took them by train from Harold Wood to Chadwell Heath, blissfully unaware that we were not supposed to use public transport for POWs."

There was then a one-mile walk from the station to Kingsley Hall Centre during which many people saw the group of six prisoners accompanied by two other young men walking through Dagenham on that Christmas morning. By the time they reached their destination, the prisoners had been given about one hundred cigarettes, and no unkind word had been spoken.

Arthur felt some emotion as he led the visitors into the packed hall for the Christmas service, during which a baby was christened, and there were tears in the prisoners' eyes. The visitors were almost overwhelmed by the welcome they received when, at the end of the service, each prisoner was taken home by a family. The fair-haired young man who had winked at Arthur that morning, Berthold Seidel, became Arthur's guest for the day.

A third step in building bridges resulted from these Christmas Day visits. Berthold Seidel became a link between his camp mates and the Kingsley Hall group. Arthur was a frequent visitor to the camp to discuss social activities between the prisoners and Kingsley Hall.

Some of the letters the prisoners received from home were heart-rending as the appalling conditions in post-war Germany became known. This led to the next step in building a bridge of friendship. Food and a great deal of clothing were collected in Dagenham and sent to various parts of Europe, through the London organisation "Save Europe Now". In fact Dagenham managed to send half a ton of clothing to a relief centre near Düsseldorf. This enterprise grew to such an extent that Arthur was summoned to the Foreign Office and asked whether Dagenham would like to consider adopting a town in Germany. Here was a further step in Arthur's dream of building a bridge of friendship between the two countries. The Dagenham/Witten exchange began, a story which Arthur Durrant told in his book, *The Two Town Story*.

35. Stamps and a Musical Christmas Card

Brian Tighe was a 17-year-old schoolboy in his last year at Middleton Grammar School, Lancashire in the autumn of 1946. His father had served as a young soldier of the First World War in the Manchester Regiment but had soon been captured and become a prisoner of war in Germany. Now, nearly 30 years later, Mr Tighe decided to invite two German prisoners of war to spend Christmas Day with his family, a decision probably based on his own memories of Germany where he felt he had been well looked after and kindly treated as a prisoner.

A little before Christmas, Mr Tighe visited the POW camp at Knutsford in Cheshire to see the camp Commandant and make arrangements. On Christmas morning he again went to the camp and collected the men, Paul Ryschawy and Alfred Birke. Paul was aged 21 and Alfred a married man in his thirties. As Mr Tighe spoke a small amount of German, and Paul had been trying to learn some English with the help of newspapers and a dictionary, some verbal communication was possible. The visitors shared in a traditional Christmas dinner with Mr and Mrs Tighe and their teenage son and 12-year-old daughter, and were introduced to the family's friends and immediate neighbours.

Mr Tighe senior (middle) visiting Brigitte and Paul Ryschawy in Germany in 1959

So memorable was this experience of Christmas hospitality to the prisoners, that it was never forgotten. Paul wrote in a letter to Brian 50 years later, "Now it is 50 years ago I spent Christmas in your father's family. I'll never forget the days in your house and the delicious roasted goose your mother served."

After repatriation, Paul was keen to keep in contact with the Tighe family. As a stamp collector,

Brian was delighted when he sent him a sheet bearing all the postage stamps in use in Germany, franked to mark the Prime Ministers' Conference of 8 June 1947, held in Munich, now a treasured part of his stamp collection (see colour photographs). Two brightly coloured cups and saucers from Bavaria, were sent to Brian's parents and are still in the family. Even today, Brian's wife, Millicent, places a large candle in a brass candleholder each Christmas. The holder, which was another present from Germany is verdigris in colour, in the shape of a snake which coils round to form a handle.

Paul Ryschawy and Brian Tighe in Karlsruhe in 1987

In 1959 Mr Tighe travelled on his own to stay with Paul and his wife Brigitte in Germany, and in 1964 Mr and Mrs Tighe went there together. Then Paul and Brigitte came to visit their English friends in Middleton, not forgetting to go to Knutsford to see the site of the POW camp.

After this, the visits started to include the second generation of both families. In 1979 Paul's 16-year-old daughter, Ingrid, spent several days with Brian and Millicent at their home in Bury, Lancashire, following a visit to see a pen friend in Scotland. During a holiday in Switzerland in 1980, Brian and Millicent paid a brief visit to Germany for the first time, meeting Paul in Karlsruhe. Next, Ingrid brought her friend Marianne to see Brian and Millicent, during a bicycle tour of Britain and Ireland. Then, in 1987, Brian and Millicent went to stay in Karlsruhe with Paul and Brigitte for a two-week holiday. They met Paul's elder daughter, Andrea, for the first time, and Paul's mother in her 90th year.

Paul now lives on his own but still keeps in touch with his English friends, sending letters, holiday postcards and Christmas cards. At Christmas 1997 a musical card arrived in Bury, playing the tune "Silent Night", a reminder of Christmas after the war, when British and German people movingly sang the well-known carol together.

Stamps, presents, photographs, letters and the musical Christmas card are all reminders of the friendship started by his father, which Brian and his wife have been pleased to continue for over half a century.

36. Somewhere to Call Home

People first settled in St Albans in the Celtic Iron Age: in the first century A.D. the settlement was given the name Verulamium by the Romans. It acquired its modern name in the third century when a young man of the town, Alban, gave shelter to Amphibalus, a Christian priest fleeing persecution. Influenced by the priest's teaching, Alban himself became a Christian. As a punishment for exchanging clothes with the priest to facilitate his escape, and then for refusing to sacrifice to Roman gods, Alban was sentenced to death by beheading.

In USA in 1944

In the eighth century the Venerable Bede wrote about St Alban, "When the peace of Christian times was restored, a beautiful church worthy of his martyrdom was built, where sick folk are healed and frequent miracles take place to this day." In the Middle Ages such large numbers of people made pilgrimages to the church that it became the most important abbey in England. The Cathedral and Abbey Church of St Alban, and the city itself, continue to attract visitors and tourists, and, as a residential area only 25 miles from London, it is considered by many to be a most desirable place to live.

Into the town of St Albans in July 1947 came a young man just 21 years of age, Gotthard Liebich, needing work. He had started life in Silesia, where his forebears had lived for several centuries, but the houses in his village had been burned by the Russians and his mother had been expelled by the Poles. This happened while Gotthard was fighting for the German army, and now he found himself a prisoner in Britain with no home to which to return.

Gotthard was greatly in need of somewhere to settle down. Since his capture by the Americans on 7 June 1944 in Normandy he had been moved around from one camp to another. First he was in England, based in Wiltshire and Northumberland. Next he was taken from Liverpool across the Atlantic, landing in Boston, and was put to work in a place called Opelika in Alabama, and Miami in Florida. He felled trees and picked cotton in Opelika from June to October 1944, and then for a further 18 months he washed dishes in Miami hotels taken over by the American army, cleared up after two hurricanes, picked

Gotthard Liebich, seated second from left, with fellow prisoners at Batford Camp, Hertfordshire, 16 June 1946

potatoes and was involved in landscaping at the airport. After the war ended he fully expected to be released but found himself being sent back to Britain, arriving in Hertfordshire at Batford Camp near Harpenden, a few miles north of St Albans, in May 1946. At first accommodation was in tents and very primitive, but later brick barracks were built.

As a prisoner of war, Gotthard had to take what work he could. Often he found it tedious, for instance when he was hoeing fields, picking potatoes, laying drainage pipes or clearing snow for three months in the bad spring of 1947. To supplement income, Gotthard and his comrades used their initiative. Jute sacks could easily be found in farm buildings, and these were smuggled into the camp and made into slippers after the lengthy business of unpicking the sacks and plaiting the strands. As footwear was still rationed, slippers were easily sold to members of the public for between 5 and 10 shillings a pair.

Gotthard remembers another effort to obtain something for nothing which this time was thwarted. Spotting some beautiful apple trees laden with fruit in a garden near Wheathampstead, Gotthard and his friend began to fill their pockets until they noticed a very old gentleman with white hair, walking with a stick slowly towards them. Only many years later did Gotthard realise that it was George Bernard Shaw, the dramatist, in person. Gotthard says, "It was GBH himself who had nearly caught me. I have revisited his house and the garden in Ayot St Lawrence since and checked on the apple trees!"

The work which Gotthard really wanted was to become part of a team of dustmen in St Albans, a gang of 12, plus driver and mate, which was already complete. Gotthard's friend Horst spoke schoolboy English

Gotthard Liebich at Lemsford Hostel near St Albans in 1947

and so had managed to obtain a job in the camp office. Gotthard implored Horst to use what influence he had in the office to get him the first vacancy which arose on the dustmen gang. So at last he replaced the first member of the group to be released early to return to Germany. It was July 1947 when Gotthard became a member of the privileged St Albans gang, and over 50 years later he is still living and working in St Albans. At last he had found somewhere to work and somewhere to call home.

Although fraternisation with members of the public had been allowed since the previous December, it was still frowned upon by many. If you understood and spoke only a little of their language, it was difficult to get to know people. Nevertheless Gotthard managed to make an important contact: it came about like this. The English driver and his mate from the dustmen's gang stopped each morning in Verulam Road at Jack's Cafe to buy the men a cup of tea. At the café was a 17-year-old waitress whom Gotthard was keen to get to know. He wrote notes which were furtively passed to her by the driver. After two failed attempts to rendezvous they met for the first time in the village of Lemsford near the school entrance, about one mile from the Hostel where Gotthard was now living. Gotthard Liebich was 21; Audrey Huitson was 17.

Gotthard's memories of those days are all good. He can honestly say that he and his comrades were treated very kindly by most people. Even so, the thing which they all wanted to do was get home, and Gotthard was at last released in October 1947. He could have stayed in Britain and kept his job, but, against Audrey's wishes and pleadings, he felt impelled to return to the continent to see his family, all of whom had been expelled from their home in Silesia, leaving everything behind.

His father had died before the war, but he had two older brothers

Audrey Huitson and Gotthard Liebich (while still a prisoner) in the fields near Borehamwood, Autumn 1947

and a younger sister. In June 1945 his mother had walked 120 miles to Berlin, and from there she had been sent to Magdeburg in the Russian Zone. His sister Elizabeth had managed to settle in the West of Germany; his older brother, Theo, was taken by the Poles after the war and made to work for four years in coal mines. Gotthard's second brother, Hans, was reported missing in May 1944 in the Crimea. It was not until 1997 that the family found out from the Red Cross that Hans had survived less than a year, dying of malnutrition in the Ukraine in January 1945.

In his search for his family, Gotthard was fairly successful. It was difficult to get into the Russian Zone, but, staying in the West, he managed to visit his mother for the first time in November 1947 and then again in March 1948 before returning to England. Having re-established these contacts, Gotthard now decided to return to St Albans to make it his new home with Audrey, his wife-to-be. This was not as easy as expected, and it required the intervention of the local MP, Cyril Dumpleton, before the Home Office agreed to accept Gotthard again into the country.

After two days' travel by train and boat, he arrived at Victoria Station, London, to be met by his future in-laws. After the wedding on 6 July 1948, Gotthard and Audrey lived with her parents in rather overcrowded conditions until St Albans Council granted them a two-up and two-down house for 37 shillings and six pence rent per week. The pavement led straight into the front room and the toilet was at the end of a small back yard. There was no electricity, no gas, no bathroom and just a cold water tap at bucket height in the kitchen. Gotthard had resumed work at Sandridge Road Depot as a dustman for five guineas a week, a job which proved invaluable for improving his house. Many items thrown away by other people found their way into his St Albans home at 47 Adelaide Street, including for instance a china kitchen sink which he stood on a sewing machine floor-stand.

After a year, Gotthard looked for work which would give him time to study each day. The ideal job was as a milkman. With a horse and cart he worked from about 6 am to 2 pm, often seven days a week. This allowed him afternoons and evenings to study by correspondence course. His first horse, Bob, knew the round better than he did and would go to the end of each road before turning round, even if the occupant of the last house was on holiday and did not need milk. One day, being engrossed in his French

As a milkman with "Bob" in 1950

vocabulary book, Gotthard had only one hand on the reins. The cart hit a deep hole, and the horse bolted, throwing Gotthard off the little step at the back of the car and landing him amidst a pile of broken bottles. The boss, Mr James Baum, a freeman of the city of St Albans, did not penalise Gotthard, and it was soon forgotten. Shortly afterwards milk floats were motorised. In the same year, 1951, Gotthard passed his Matriculation Examination, but, with a growing family of three children by this time, he regretfully had to give up his milk round after seven years, part way towards a degree, to concentrate on earning more money.

Gotthard was always a hard worker so in 1959, when he was made redundant, he decided to start his own wholesale business in electrical and radio spare parts, moving on to hi-fi and electronic components. When the Beatles became popular many of his lines exceeded all expectations. In the 1960s he opened two retail shops, one in Kensington and the other in St Albans, and his wholesale business spread to other parts of the country. For 20 years Gotthard's enterprises flourished though it meant his working over 80 hours per week.

Calamity struck when his trusted sales representative was found to have misappropriated money, resulting in arrest and prosecution and affecting Gotthard's trust in people. Two of his children, Marion and Peter, joined the business to try and keep it going after this severe setback, and then Audrey was taken ill with breast cancer. Soon afterwards Gotthard had a nervous breakdown, spending six weeks in hospital. He sums up those times with these words, "We were blessed with five healthy children, and I now have six grandchildren. We celebrated our silver wedding in style in 1973. Sadly my Audrey succumbed to the dread-

Taking parcels through the snow to each house in Krolkwitz in December 1981

ful breast cancer disease, and she had to leave our seemingly happy, content and well-off family on 21 December 1975." In the 1970s, Gotthard suffered two more break-downs and had to sell his business at below market value but later regained his health.

Mr Liebich is not the sort of person to retire and put his feet up. During the Polish food crisis of 1981 and 1982 he made the decision to help his old home village of Krolkwitz, now renamed Kroliko-wice by the Poles. His plan was to take food, clothes, shoes and medicine to the people now living there, even though they were complete strangers to him. He and his second daughter, Marion, borrowed a van and set off for Poland 14 days after martial law had been declared there (due to the Solidarnosze troubles), and three days after Christmas 1981, in very cold and snowy weather. They went through seven border crossings each way, including East/West German borders. When they arrived they distributed the contents of the van equally to each house in the two villages of Krolkwitz and Beitsch. Gotthard recalls the reaction and his response in these words:

Gotthard Liebich glad to be back home safely from Poland in March 1982, with the van lent freely by Countryside Truck Hire

Everyone there was completely stunned. Encouraged by this success I went on a second mercy trip with a friend in February 1982, with a much larger lorry to the same area, and also to other parts of southwest Poland. I now have many friends there.

He also had friends and relations in the German Democratic Republic. One of his trips there happened to be at the time of the fall of the Berlin Wall. At exactly midnight on 9 November 1989 he stood on the platform of the Friedrichstrasse underground station. It was a momentous occasion for the thousands of people in Berlin as well as for millions of others in the world who welcomed the unification of Germany. Gotthard was there to experience it for himself.

Although St Albans is home to Mr Liebich, he cannot forget his original home in Silesia. He has made contact with others who came from the same area and together they have journeyed from various parts of Europe to their home villages. Mr Liebich is the one who has arranged these visits, the travel and the hospitality. The first trip was by bus in 1995, the 50th anniversary of the expulsion of the population of Silesia by the Poles. There were 54 in the party, including homeland friends, their spouses, children and, in some cases, even grandchildren. The second bus trip was of 47 people in 1998, and the third was of 40 friends who stayed a week in the villages in the summer of 2001. Each trip was very much appreciated by all the visitors and also by many of the people now living in the villages.

Mr Liebich has also put his communication and administrative skills to good use in another way. He has made it his business to try to contact any former prisoners of war who chose to do as he did, and make their home in Britain. He visits as many as possible of these men and their wives

*Group visit to Krolkwitz in July 2001. Singing German folk songs,
sitting in a field formerly owned by Gotthard Liebich's Uncle Gustav*

and widows, writes to them and sends a "round robin" letter every so often.
This self-imposed task does not provide many rewards as some of the
people on the list die each year and others are too old or ill to reply. In
1999 Mr Liebich wrote, "I now have 112 comrades including some widows
and even children of ex-POWs, plus other local comrades I see from time
to time and about 50 names and addresses I have not yet contacted. Just
how much work I have given myself, voluntarily of course, nobody can
imagine. My wish to visit as many as possible as I travel around the country
has enabled me so far to make 45 visits." Mr Liebich comments in one of
his round robin letters, "Just remember that we all started with next to
nothing, just a lot of determination. Only hard work saw most of us through
life." He then lists some of the achievements of the former prisoners he
has met, from the man who worked for 20 years in the German Embassy to
the one who sold his business for a million pounds (see colour photographs).

The fact that Mr Liebich chose to make St Albans his home has been
acknowledged by the city itself. In 1998 one hundred personalities from
St Albans were selected to commemorate the museum's centenary. Gotthard Liebich was honoured to be chosen to represent the large POW
community in the city and surrounding area. His story, along with a POW's
outfit, was featured in the seven-month-long exhibition in the museum
(see colour photographs).

Most of the stories in this book are about friendships between German
prisoners and their former "enemies". This story is about a friendship
with a city. The city of St Albans became the place where a prisoner
needing refuge found somewhere to call Home.

Acknowledgements

The author acknowledges the generous and meticulous help of the following people who freely provided detailed information and treasured illustrations for this book.

1. Margaret Smith
2. Tony Bischoff, Jim Cranton, Rosemary Ottery, Helmut Heilmann, Arthur Harris, John White, Rev. Richard Terrell; Photographs: Brenda Bickerton
3. George and Herbert Harder
4. Horst Alexander
5. Jeffrey Hine
6. Helmut Eckardt
7. Renée Longson
8. Ernst Siebels, Jack Adams, Malcolm Dennett
9. Peter Spencer, Ursula Klein
10. David Hall
11. Margaret Smith, Johannes Baumann, Dr W R Mitchell
12. Dorothy Blandford
13. Dr George M Betts
14. Stefan and Dorothy Bolz
15. Christine and David Harding, Rolf Göhler
16. Marian Claassen Franz
17. Ernest Clarke
18. Peter Knight, Willi Wontroba, Peggy Taylor
19. Renate Greenshields
20. John Gaunt, Günther Scheffler, Dr Wolf Berlin, Colonel Myrddin Jones, Wolfgang Berghoff, Rev. Friedrich Wilhelm Wandersleb
21. Ann Croker
22. Brian Tucker, Harald Beiersdorf, Michael Fox, Penelope Putz
23. Iris Gardner, Elsie Duxbury
24. Peter Roth
25. Rev. Hugh Knapman, Audrey Newman, Ivy Mitchell, Rev. Beverley Tasker
26. Clemens Schwertmann, Gerald Towell
27. Jean Degurse. Photograph: Josephine Zell
28. Fritz Defèr, Gerald Towell
29. Greta Browning, Fritz Kübler, Peter Heathfield
30. Kurt Geibel, Paul and Kathleen Johnson
31. Keith Spittlehouse, Hugh and Marjorie Williams
32. Peter Heathfield, Dr Winfried Fischer, Claude-Alain Danthe
33. Noreen Almond
34. Christine and David Harding
35. Brian Tighe
36. Gotthard Liebich

Script readers: Lawrence Taylor, Josephine Zell

Further Reading

Enemies Become Friends by Pamela Howe Taylor. The Book Guild, 1997, reprinted 1998. Using letters, diaries and newspaper reports left by her father, the author tells a moving and well illustrated story of unexpected friendships developing between German prisoners and British people. It formed the basis of award-winning television and radio programmes in Britain and Germany. Last few books now available only from the author at Cleadon, Weston, Honiton, Devon, EX14 3PQ, England. £6.95 plus £1 postage within UK.
E-mail: Pamela9939@aol.com
Web site: http://members.aol.com/pamela9939

A Cornish Rhapsody: From a Penny Halfpenny an hour to a Fortune, auto-biography by Rudi Mock, ex-POW who makes good in Britain. Mounts Bay Press, 2001. £11 including postage from the author at Woodland Lodge, Station Hill, Praze, Camborne, TR14 0JE, England.

Letter of a Lifetime by Franz Münchow, story of ex-POW who settled in Scotland, as told in a letter to his daughter, Jane. Dunbar Publications, 1999. £9.95 from Mrs Jane McCarthy, 42 Salters Road, Gosforth, NE3 1DX, England. Available in German or English.

Freedom in Captivity by S.G. Mohring. Personal recollections of World War Two including youth in Germany, time in the front line, years as a POW in England, English friends and lifelong friendships. Books on Demand GmbH, 2001. £10 including postage from the author at Graf Rhena Strasse 17, 76137 Karlsruhe, Germany. Available in German or English. E-mail enquiries: s.g.mohring@t-online.de

Lucky Girl Goodbye by Renate Greenshields. Growing up in pre-war Germany, Hitler Youth, living through the war in Germany and falling in love with an English Major. Minerva Press, 1995. £8.99 including postage within UK, from the author at Westhay Farm, Hawkchurch, Axminster, EX13 5XH, England.

From Pomerania to Ponteland, 2001, by Rudi Lux who claims to be the youngest prisoner of war in Britain at sixteen. He describes his youth in Pomerania, his six weeks in the German army and his three years in POW camps in the northeast of England, after which he settled down in Ponteland, Northumberland. £5.50 including postage within UK from Rudi Lux at 25 Ferneybeds Estate, Widdrington, Morpeth, NE61 5RD, England.

Index

People are listed only if they occur in more than one story, or are well-known names. The numbers refer to the story number rather than the page.